THE BUSINESS OF AMERICAN INJUSTICE

Sydney Williams

DEDICATION

My trials brought me to my faith and the love of God.
I have more joy in my life now, than ever before.
My wife, Lorie walked with me thru the hardest times of our
marriage, she kept me from drowning, she is a gift to me from the
heavens above…..

I dedicate this book to my very best friend,
the love of my life……Bean
My wife, Lorie.

I LOVE YOU!

THE BUSINESS OF AMERICAN INJUSTICE
PROLOGUE

Regardless of political persuasion, we, as Americans, want to believe that the law protects the weak from the strong, and every citizen from his own government. As Americans, we want to know whether the Justice Department has been biased and corrupted. We have an obligation to find out whether it is putting people in positions of power who are so biased they should not be a part of the Department of Justice. Are the people in power more interested in padding their own resumes and bending the law for their own self-serving interests?

The story I am about to tell shows a side of America's legal system that is something quite different from what the Founding Fathers intended.

The Constitution establishes three branches of government, balance of powers, and the doctrine of federalism which governs the relationship between the states and the federal government. The Constitution mentions only three criminal offenses:

1. Piracy

2. Counterfeiting

3. Treason

There are 4,543 words in the original US constitution. We now have almost 5,000 criminal offenses. One in every 263 people we encounter is a lawyer. We have over 25% of the world's prisoners. Vague and absurd laws create lawbreakers. More such laws create more law breakers.

Harvey A. Silvergate wrote "Three Felonies a Day. How the Feds Target the Innocent." He states that the average professional in this country goes to work, comes home, eats dinner and then goes to sleep unaware that he or she has likely committed several federal crimes that day.

Have you ever told someone a true story, after which, their only comment was, "You just made that up, didn't you?"

This is a story about our personal journey through civil litigation, bankruptcy, and the criminal justice system. As unbelievable as it seems, each event is a matter of public record. The frightening reality is that it could happen to you.

Our story is a tribute to the strength of our relationship. We lost all our money. We experienced forced separation because of incarceration, for an offense with no victims. After all of that, our bond to each other remains strong.

This is also a story about our spiritual journey and why forgiveness is so important. Carrying unforgiveness in your heart does not allow the healing process to begin or the opportunity to experience peace and joy.

Joel Osteen wrote in "Fresh Start" that "Unforgiveness is like drinking poison and expecting the other person to die". It only hurts you.

Our journey has shown me that you never truly know yourself, or the strength of your friendships, until both have been tested by adversity.

CHAPTER 1

I NEVER THOUGHT I WOULD WRITE A BOOK. THE thought had never occurred to me.

If not for the prompting from many of my close friends, it would never have happened. After every bizarre legal experience, someone would invariably say, "You should write a book. No one would believe it."

One of my closest friends told me "the system hasn't served you well." That could be the understatement of the century. It's like the mayor of Hiroshima saying, "did anyone else hear that?"

Before we embark on our journey, I think it is important to share with anyone who might read this book a little about my background. I grew up with mid-western values in Indiana.

I was born in July 1948 in Anderson, Indiana. My mother used to say "postwar- pre-pill." My mother and father were 22 years old when I was born.

My father had served in the Navy and graduated with a chemistry degree from Indiana University. He received his Doctor of Pharmacy degree from Butler University. After a brief career as a pharmaceutical salesman, my father bought a neighborhood drugstore which he owned for 35 years.

My father followed in the footsteps of my grandfather, who graduated from Purdue School of Pharmacy in 1917. My grandfather owned a downtown drugstore in Anderson, Indiana for 50 years.

My grandfather had trained to run track and field in the 1916 Olympics, but they were canceled because of the war. Upon graduation, he enlisted in the army and served in Germany until the war ended. When the armistice sounded, ending the war, he was lying in a trench in Alsace-Lorraine. Had the war not ended, I might not be writing this book

My mother worked one year as a telephone operator but, otherwise, remained a homemaker who raised my younger sister and me. We lived an upper- middle-class existence with strong family ties and a strong work ethic.

I graduated from high school in 1966. I attended Ball State University in Muncie, Indiana, and graduated with a Bachelor of Science degree in Business Administration in 1972. After my sophomore year, I worked two jobs, six nights a week, tending bar. They were the best jobs I ever had.

I enlisted in the US Army reserves in 1968 and received an honorable discharge in 1974. I served my active duty at Fort Leonard Wood, Missouri.

In 1974, I thought I should probably try to get a real job. I applied to, and was hired at, Ford Motor Company in Connersville, Indiana. I started as a quality control supervisor and was later promoted to Industrial Relations Supervisor. I spent some time in Salary Personnel. I was offered the position of Senior Industrial Relations Supervisor over the salaried union personnel who provided information to Jet Propulsion Laboratories in California. The position would have required me to move to Barstow, California. I turned it down.

In 1977, I was asked to be the administrator of the first unionized long-term care facility in Newcastle, Indiana because they were experiencing severe labor problems. As an incentive to leave Ford Motor Company, they offered me an equity position in the company.

I left Ford Motor Company in February of 1977 and went back to school to obtain my Health Facility Administrator license.

After operating the facility for almost a year, I formed a partnership and began acquiring additional long-term care facilities throughout Indiana.

In 1985 and 1986, we sold all the facilities and I retired for the first time.

I bought a condo in Naples, Florida where my parents were living by this time. After about six months, I became bored and saw an opportunity to acquire commercial shopping centers. I formed another partnership and acquired numerous multi-tenant commercial properties throughout Indiana.

The ability to acquire these commercial properties came from the equity provided by various investors. Many were lifelong friends. Fortunately, all the properties were successful and provided good returns to the investors.

In the mid to late 90s, I sold all the commercial properties in Indiana and retired again. Obviously, I don't retire well because, after a short while, I saw another opportunity to acquire single-tenant industrial properties throughout the United States.

In the late 90s, I formed a business alliance with two companies out of Chicago and began to syndicate these commercial properties.

Once again, the equity to acquire these properties was provided by the same numerous investors from the 1980s, as well as from new relationships I had established in Florida.

All the commercial properties we acquired were cash flowing and paying quarterly dividend distributions to our investors. We had acquired several million square feet of property in a relatively short period of time. All the investments had been successful, and all the projected investor dividend projections had been met. It was not until the end of 2008 and the beginning of 2009, when the economy collapsed, that we started to realize some tenant problems.

Fortunately, our portfolio consisted of quality tenants, many of whom were investment-grade. Dow Chemical, Hartford Insurance, AON, Heinz, General Electric and Caterpillar, to name a few. As a result, we experienced only a small percentage of defaults, relative to the number of properties in our portfolio.

CHAPTER 2

"For a long, long time it had seemed to me that I was about to begin a real- life.

But there was always some obstacle in the way, something to be gotten through first,

some unfinished business, time still to be served, a debt to be paid. Then life would begin. At last it dawned on me that these obstacles were my life."

— Alfred Souza

MOST OF MY CAREER EXPERIENCE HAS BEEN IN commercial real estate. Even when we operated the long-term care facilities in Indiana, we owned the real estate. I know how to analyze real estate values and investments.

Capitol Investments was not in a business with which I was familiar. When I was introduced to Capitol Investments in 2002, I had a number of questions.

Capitol Investments had been operating for several years as a diverter of food products and was looking for additional capital. Capitol Investments purchased food products from major manufacturers. The products were to be redistributed out of the country. The manufacturers offered significant discounts to compensate for the costs of exporting. In addition, there was a 2 to 3% discount for paying for the products upfront rather than under 60 to 90-day terms.

A significant portion of the products purchased were actually resold in the United States. The manufactures didn't move significant amounts of their inventory, especially in the fourth quarter of each year. I was told that, because of the discounts, Capitol Investments could sell Pringles potato chips to local stores cheaper than the stores could buy directly from the manufacturer. This was confirmed by an executive I talked with at Procter& Gamble.

I confirmed the legitimacy of this business with executives at Procter& Gamble and ConAgra. They confirmed that the diverting practice was common and, in fact, a multibillion dollar per year industry.

Based on my research of the industry, and in no small part upon the recommendation from my longtime friend, I agreed to make an original capital investment of $500,000. This note would follow a specific transaction in which product was sold. The term of the Note was 30 days. The transaction, I was told, would be completed within this period. The Note would be personally guaranteed by Nevin Shapiro, and by Capitol Investments, USA, Inc.

At the end of 30 days, 100% of the investment was to be returned, with the agreed upon interest under the terms of the Note.

At the end of 30 days, all the requirements of the Note were met. The principal was returned, along with a profit equal to a 10% annualized return.

CHAPTER 3

MANY OF MY REGULAR REAL ESTATE INVESTORS looked to me to identify other alternative investment opportunities. Once I identified opportunities, many of the investors would seek advice from their own financial advisors with respect to these opportunities. This investor group included many sophisticated and connected investors.

Capitol Investments was an investment opportunity unlike real estate.

Real estate investments are illiquid compared to Capitol Investments' short turnaround period which was, typically, 30 to 45 days. The products purchased by Capitol were already in transit. The products purchased were already resold to various retail chains throughout the country.

Before I felt comfortable recommending Capitol to friends as an alternative investment opportunity, I tried to become better acquainted with the company's financials and track record. I continued to make personal investments in Capitol Investments for the next several months. I reviewed the bank statements, financial statements, and tax returns that were provided to me.

After approximately 6 months of successful returns, I was comfortable with the results of this business. I approached one of our long-term real estate investors and told him about Capitol

Investments. Explaining what I knew of the company, the industry in general, and the positive experience I had had over the last six months. We agreed to form a partnership to invest in Capitol.

Over the next several months, the two of us made multiple investments that were generally for periods of 30 to 60 days. Capitol met all its financial obligations.

In the second year, we were asked to make a more substantial investment. Shapiro told us there was an opportunity to lock in substantial profits if we could make a financial commitment for a period of three years rather than investing in a single particular sale. Capitol offered a longer-term commitment to buy products from its suppliers. Capitol offered to amortize the entire note over 36 months. The requested loan amount was $3.5 million dollars.

This required more liquidity than our two-man partnership had available. Because of Capitol's track record and positive financials, we decided to offer part of this opportunity to some of our real estate investors. Because of the dollar amount, I engaged the accounting firm of RSM McGladrey to go to Miami to perform an audit of Capitol's books. I wanted confirmation that Capitol could, in fact, make the amortized payments over the 36-month period.

McGladrey spent three days in Miami conducting the audit. Its conclusion was that Capitol had the resources available to amortize the entire note over 36 months.

Based on that analysis, I reached out to six additional investors. We collectively funded the requested $3.5 million.

Over the next three years, all the amortized payments were made on time. As the payments were being made, word spread among our other investors that Capitol appeared to be a more liquid investment opportunity than our traditional net- leased real estate investments provided. As additional short-term investments in Capitol became available, we offered them to many of our longtime real estate investors. Capitol continued to provide favorable financial statements, bank statements, and tax returns.

One of our sophisticated real estate investment contacts in Chicago formed an investment entity to provide his numerous real estate investors the opportunity to invest in Capitol.

It wasn't until the end of 2008, and the first quarter of 2009, that Capitol was starting to experience problems. Scheduled payments were late. Shapiro blamed the economy. When Capitol was no longer meeting its financial obligations, the Chicago partnership placed Capitol into involuntary bankruptcy. A bankruptcy trustee was appointed.

Once the bankruptcy trustee became involved, he told us that Capitol, for the last several years, had been operating as a Ponzi scheme. His books, records, financial statements, and tax returns had been fabricated to convey to the investors that Capitol was performing as represented.

We discovered that Capitol had been under investigation by the United States Justice Department in New Jersey. One of Capitol's major suppliers had been operating out of New Jersey and had apparently prompted the investigation. This investor, including me, invested and lost millions more after the FBI and U S Attorney's office knew that Shapiro was a fraud and Capitol investments was a Ponzi scheme.

CHAPTER 4

———

IT HAS BEEN DIFFICULT FOR ME TO DETERMINE exactly when Capitol became a target of the Justice Department. It appears that the Justice Department began investigating Capitol sometime in 2005. Prior to 2005, Capitol had been operating as a legitimate business. In 2005, Shapiro began making investments outside the scope of his primary business. Poor real estate investments and compulsive gambling issues contributed to his problems. I wasn't involved in or aware of these issues. In June 2011, Shapiro was sentenced to 20 years in prison.

Because the government had been investigating Capitol for several years, they were aware of my personal involvement as a large investor, and in introducing numerous investors to Capitol. I was approached in 2010 by the US Attorney's Office in Newark to come to New Jersey and answer questions. The FBI wanted to know how I had learned about Capitol and how I understood Capitol operated.

The FBI told my attorneys that I was not a "person of interest "in the Ponzi scheme. The government wanted to meet with me to get further insight into Capitol Investments. I flew to New Jersey and met with the assistant US Attorney and members of the FBI and Internal Revenue Service. I explained how I was introduced to Capitol and my history with the company. I explained my understanding of the food diverting industry, and how Capitol was supposed to be running. The meeting was not confrontational. Everyone was very polite and seemed genuinely interested in my perception of how Capitol operated.

After our meeting, the agent representing the IRS indicated that a review of my tax returns and Capitol's records appeared to reflect an inaccurate reporting of income. I suggested that the agents travel to Indianapolis and meet with my accountants. I offered to make available all my books and records for their review. My returns were very complicated, because my business involved numerous, single tenant real estate entities throughout the United States. I had to file state returns in 12 to14 states. My accounting firm in Indianapolis was one of the largest in the country. They had been preparing my returns since the late 1970s.

CHAPTER 5

———

THE IRS SPENT SEVERAL DAYS WITH MY ACCOUN-
tants. The IRS disagreed with my accountants about the amount of
money we had claimed as "return of capital", they stated it should
have been "income." By the end of 2008, I had outstanding loans to
Capitol Investments greater than $10 million dollars. They became
uncollectible when Capitol Investments collapsed. Prior to 2008, I
had claimed a portion of the money I received under these loans as
a return of my principal, instead of interest.

I had paid more than $3 million dollars in federal taxes for the
years 2004-2007. In 2008 and 2009, I had net operating losses that
resulted in carryback refunds. I used most of the refund proceeds
to pay off the first and second mortgages on our personal residence.

After several days of meetings, the government agreed that a
portion of this money I received from Capitol was "return of capital".
The IRS still disputed the balance.

The IRS's position was that I had "signed an inaccurate tax
return". They wanted me to acknowledge such by entering into a
negotiated plea agreement. The government pointed out that my
wife had signed the return as well, because we filed a joint return.
I agreed to a negotiated plea agreement in return for the IRS agreement not to pursue any action against my wife.

On September 27, 2011, I pled guilty to" subscribing to a false tax return" in the United States District Court in Newark, N.J.

I do not believe that most people are naïve about the law. They know that it can be perverted to serve a host of causes other than justice. We have a legal system geared to enhancing legal, and sometimes political, careers. It often operates by setting examples to instill fear or unquestioning compliance.

I have never filed a lawsuit against anyone in my life. I have always taken personal responsibility for my actions. I have been disappointed by the number of people who do not. Rather than assume personal responsibility, they find it easier to blame someone else. I've had several opportunities in my lifetime to receive a personal benefit by blaming others. I have never done so. This day was no exception.

I am reminded of a poem I learned from my grandfather titled "The Man in the Glass". I have always tried to live by it.

> "*When life grants you wishes in your struggle for self, and you accept many cheers in your day,*
>
> *Go look in the glass at the jolly old elf, find out just what he has to say.*
>
> *He's the one you live with, disregard all the rest,*
>
> *For alas in the end, you've passed your most difficult test,*
>
> *If the man in the glass was your friend.*
>
> *It's not family judgment that you have to pass, For the fellow's verdict that counts most,*
>
> *Is the one staring back in the glass.*
>
> *Yes, you may baffle the world down through the years, get cheers and pats on your back as you pass,*
>
> *But your reward will only be heartache and tears, if you cheated the man in the glass.*"

On January 10th, 2012, I was sentenced to one year and one day in federal prison to be followed by one year of supervised release. I was fined $25,000. I was released on my own recognizance. I would be told where and when to report. We all returned to Florida.

CHAPTER 6

———

FOR THE FIRST TIME, I WAS CONFRONTED WITH the reality that I would soon be going to federal prison. My only prior experience with the criminal justice system was when I received a $50 citation for not wearing my seatbelt.

To get some insight into what to expect, my attorneys engaged the services of a prison consultant. He had been a former judge who spent 10 years in prison and now told people what to expect. While he did not know where I would be required to report, he knew that I would be housed with individuals who have been in the prison system for a long time. Many of the inmates would have been in numerous other facilities. Only when they have 10 years or less left to serve on their sentences are they eligible to be assigned to a satellite camp facility.

Because many of the inmates would have been born between 1945 and 1965, and had a history of using injectable drugs, the prison consultant felt it was important that I get hepatitis C injections before I reported. Hepatitis C is a disease that affects the liver. It is caused by the hepatitis C virus, which is spread through contact with the blood of an infected person.

Taking his advice, I went to a walk-in clinic, talked with a physician assistant and asked to be treated. He said it would be no problem. The treatment would require three different injections. One could be administered that day.

Another would be required in 30 days. A third would be required in three months.

I told him that there was no problem with the first two but that I would not be available for the third in three months. He asked if I was going on vacation. I said, "No, I'm going to federal prison." He said, "No you're not." I said, "Yes, unfortunately, that's the truth." He asked, "Why?" I told him that I had signed an inaccurate tax return. He asked, "Where do you have to go?" I said, "I have no idea." He asked, "When do you have to report?" I said, "I'm not sure, but I know I won't be here in three months." "If that's the case," he said, "how do you know where and when you are supposed to report?" I told him that I would be receiving a letter in the mail with instructions on when and where to report. He said, "That's unbelievable." I should get the doctor. "He's got to hear this." I repeated the same story for the attending physician. He said he would give me a prescription to take with me for the final injection in three months. I thanked him and left the clinic.

A few weeks later, I received a letter in the mail instructing me to self- surrender on February 14, 2012 to the federal prison in Edgefield, South Carolina.

February 14th was a Tuesday. It was Valentine's Day, and the anniversary of my engagement to my wife. We certainly had not anticipated this event.

We flew to Atlanta on Friday the 10th, and caught a connecting flight to Augusta, Georgia. Edgefield, South Carolina is approximately 25 miles from Augusta. We booked a room at a bed and breakfast. We wanted to see the town and the prison facility prior to having to report. I was supposed to be reporting to a satellite camp facility. When we drove by the facility for the first time we were shocked to see that it didn't look like a camp at all. The front looked like administrative offices, and the grounds were enclosed with a razor wire fence. I could see what looked like a walking track with an open-air pavilion off to the side. Next door, where I was told to report, was a federal penitentiary facility that housed several thousand inmates. It had eight armed -guard towers. Two security cars drove in opposite directions around the facility 24 hours a day. Some of the inmates, I was later told, had two life sentences +40 years. Obviously, security was tight.

I was required to report by noon. The prison consultant advised me to report early so that I could be processed and assigned to the camp facility as soon as possible. He said that, many times, the processing is slow and inefficient. In some instances, inmates have had to spend the night in a special housing unit known as the (SHU) before their processing was completed the next day. The SHU is a cell in solitary confinement.

Armed with this frightening scenario, I reported at 8 o'clock in the morning. My wife and I waited in the lobby until someone came to get me. This was a very emotional time. Approximately 30 minutes later, a security guard came to process me. We said our goodbyes and I told my wife I would call her as soon as possible.

I was led back through a series of rooms where bars would open electrically in front of me and, as I stepped forward, they would close behind me. Finally, we reached the room in a separate building where I was to be processed.

I was told to disrobe and place all my personal effects in a cardboard box that was provided, including the prescription I had brought for my hepatitis C shot. The guard told me they didn't offer that. I was told everything would be mailed home. I was allowed to keep only my wedding ring. I was told to bend over and spread my buttocks cheeks. He inspected my hair and looked in my mouth. I was asked to lift my testicles. He looked at the bottom of my feet. I was issued the standard jumpsuit you see on television and a pair of slippers. They took a DNA swab from inside my mouth.

After being asked several questions to determine any previous criminal history, gang affiliations, tattoos or other distinguishing marks, I was directed to a holding cell and told someone would come to take me to the camp next door. The cell had a metal bench, sink and toilet. Around noon, I was provided lunch through a slot in the door.

I cannot accurately describe what the meal was, but it was the first time I prayed after I ate.

Finally, approximately eight hours later, the door opened, and I thought it was time to leave. Instead, someone else was put in the holding cell with me.

About two hours later, a guard came to take us to the facility next door.

While we were walking next door, the guard asked us if we had a cell phone.

I thought that was a strange question because we had been stripped of all our possessions and held in a holding cell for the past 10 hours. Welcome to the BOP (Bureau of Prisons).

The BOP was established in 1930 to house federal inmates, principally to ensure consistent and centralized administration of the Federal prison system. The BOP is the largest correctional agency in the country, in terms of the number of prisoners under its jurisdiction. The BOP must confine any offender convicted and sentenced to a term of imprisonment in a federal court.

Having always worked in the private sector, where results are expected, I was astonished to see the waste and inefficiency of the BOP.

The burgeoning federal prison population has led Congress to increase appropriations for the BOP's operations and infrastructure. In fiscal year 1980, Congress appropriated $330 million for the BOP. By fiscal year 2014, the total appropriation for the BOP reached $6.859 billion dollars. The additional funding for the BOP was necessary to cover the costs of providing services to a growing prison population, expanding prison capacity, and hiring additional staff to manage the expanding federal prison system. Changes in federal criminal justice policy since the early 1980s have resulted in a continued increase in the federal prison population. The number of inmates under the BOP's jurisdiction has increased nearly eight-fold (790%) from approximately 24,600 inmates in fiscal year 1980 to nearly 219,300 inmates in fiscal year 2013. Since fiscal year 1980, the federal prison population has increased, on average, by approximately 5900 inmates each year. Unfortunately, I believe that a significant portion of this additional funding was necessary to compensate for much of the waste and inefficiency of the BOP. The specific inefficiencies are too numerous to mention but, during the course of writing this book, I will point out many.

CHAPTER 7

"If you do not take an interest in the affairs of your government, then you are doomed to live under the rule of fools."

—Plato

IN MARCH 2011, THE THEN SOON TO BE RETIRED Director of the BOP was arrested and charged with DUI and related counts after county police spotted him driving erratically near his home in Annapolis.

Harley Lappin, 55, was pulled over after a police officer watched him nearly swerve into a police speed enforcement trailer and a parked car on Headwater Road, according to a police report. Lappin's eyes were bloodshot, his speech was slurry and his breath smelled of alcohol, according to the report. A field sobriety test showed he was unable to walk a straight-line heel to toe, and he could not maintain his balance standing on one foot. Charles E Samuels Jr. was appointed director of the federal agency on December 21, 2011 by Attorney General Eric Holder. He was the eighth director since the BOP's establishment in 1930. His tenure lasted until January 9, 2016.

I encourage you to look at the YouTube video by John Oliver where Director Samuels is questioned by Senator Al Franken.

If you don't know a prisoner or think you'll ever become one, prisoner safety and health is not going to be one of your priorities. You don't need to know about any of the conditions in which they live. The Director of federal prisons, however, should know.

The following is a brief transcript from the YouTube video where director Samuels almost comically struggles to recall the most basic detail about one of the most mentally excruciating conditions to which prisoners can be subjected: solitary confinement.

"Franken: How big is a cell? How big is the average cell in solitary confinement? Samuels: You say the average size?

Franken: Yes, the average size, how big is it? Samuels: I'm trying to understand, you mean in space?

Franken: I'm trying to get---this is a human thing were talking about. We have a lot of statistics but how big is the cell?

Samuels: The average size of the cell is, I guess I'm trying to find, are you looking for the space?

Franken: Yes, the dimensions in feet and inches. The size of the cell that a person is kept in. I'm trying to get some idea I don't know, am I asking this question wrong?

John Oliver: No, as far as I can tell he's only asking him the size of the f----ing cell. But that was a long time ago. To be fair he finally did get an answer.

Samuels: The average size should be the equivalent of 6 x 4.

John Oliver: Couple of things there, that was clearly a guess. And too, 6 x 4 is barely the size of an elevator. That's the length of a six-foot party sub by the length of that party sub that's left over the following day because no one wants leftover party subs, people put their hands all over them, they're disgusting. But that's not the point."

A few moments later the record was corrected.

"Samuels: The actual size he stated is 10 x 7 for the cell size.

John Oliver: Oh 10 x 7, step this way your highness. Plenty of room for a ping- pong table and an imaginary opponent as your mind slowly becomes untethered."

This mindset should speak volumes about who is running the Country's institutional facilities. Having first-hand experience, I can tell you about the accommodations and staff at the Edgefield facility.

Because everyone in a camp facility will ultimately be going to a Residential Reentry Program, there is a constant turnover of inmates. The census varied, but the population averaged 530 to 560 inmates. There was a two story, four-unit building. One of the units was designated for RDAP which is the Residential Drug and Alcohol Program. Inmates who qualified for this program were eligible for early discharge from the facility. Generally, they were given a year off their sentence.

Units were designated D1, D2, D3 and D4. I was housed in the second story unit, D4, affectionately referred to as "the ghetto." Each unit was assigned a case manager and counselor. Each unit was an open dorm, consisting of 2 to 3 bed cubicles.

The population was approximately 50% Puerto Rican, 45% black and 5% white. I often joked that, with the exception of a few caddies, wait staff, and casino employees, the U. S. has somehow managed to incarcerate the entire commonwealth of Puerto Rico.

The guard escorting me did not take me to my unit. Instead, he handed me a blanket and some basic toiletries and told me my bed assignment was 514 L, pointing to the D4 unit located on the second floor. I was later told that, when I walked into the unit, the look on my face was priceless. For those who recall "Alice in Wonderland," I realized I had just fallen into the rabbit hole.

The scene is hard to describe. There were probably around 140 inmates housed in D4. Most appeared to be Puerto Rican. There was a lot of yelling and screaming. It was immediately apparent that English was a second language.

Almost everyone was speaking Spanish. Unfortunately, I had had three years of French and could only recall that I liked the French teacher. The decibel level seemed to be about 10 decibels over the pain threshold. It made me wonder if most people from Puerto Rico are deaf.

Fortunately, I was approached by a young Spanish inmate who saw the look of confusion on my face. He showed me to my cubicle assignment. 514 L was located immediately adjacent to the restroom. "L" stood for lower bunk to which I was assigned because of my age. This cubicle consisted of three beds. I was the only one assigned to this cubicle. The bedframe was metal and bolted to the floor. As I mentioned, I had been given a blanket, but there was no mattress on the frame. The inmate said he would try to find me one. A few minutes later, he brought me a blue pad about 2 inches thick. This was my mattress.

I was then introduced to one of the older inmates who was affiliated with a Christian group. He helped new inmates settle into their new environment. He gave me some shower shoes, bar soap, toothpaste and toothbrush. He said he would give me a tour of the unit and help me with my orientation. Because I had processed in so late, I had not eaten dinner. He introduced me to the inmate who ran the "store." Think of this person as "Red" in Shawshank redemption. He gave me a Coke and something to eat.

I was then given a tour of the rest of the dorm. There was a TV room, a card room, and a small room with four microwaves and a hot water dispenser.

The sinks, toilets and showers were located directly across from my cubicle.

The lights were turned off at 10 o'clock each night in the dorm but remained on for 24 hours in the restrooms. Unfortunately, those lights shined directly into my cubicle.

There were four phones and four computers located just inside the dorm entrance. Obviously, no one was allowed internet access but a core links account could later be set up to email, and receive emails from, an approved list of contacts.

Each inmate was allocated 300 minutes per month to call people approved on his contact list. Calls were limited to 15 minutes after which we had to wait half an hour before making another call. Calls could only be made during certain times, so there was always a long line.

Every day there are standing counts at 10 AM, 4 PM and 10 PM. Each inmate is required to be standing at his bed side during these times. There is no talking during the counts. In addition to the counts, guards come through the unit at midnight and 3 AM for additional counts. They shine a flashlight into the faces of the inmates while they are sleeping.

Because I was directly across from the bathrooms, where the light shined into my cubicle 24 hours a day, the flashlight was not necessary.

According to the BOP manual, each unit is supposed to be quiet after the 10 PM count so everyone can sleep. Nothing could be further from the truth. Most of the inmates are up all night talking loudly. It is impossible to sleep.

The next morning, I reported to the laundry where I was issued my green fatigues and steel-toed boots. I was also issued some T-shirts, and underwear.

Everyone is required to wear green fatigues from 8 AM to 4 PM. After 4 PM, we could wear shorts, sweats and T-shirts purchased in the commissary.

Everyone is assigned a specific job. Some of the inmates worked outside the facility mowing grass and doing other odd jobs in the town of Edgefield. Other inmates had jobs at a Unicore facility. I was not allowed to leave the facility grounds and was assigned the job of "compound orderly." This job paid five dollars and forty cents per month or $.18 per day. There were higher-paying jobs, but I don't recall anyone making more than $100 per month.

We could purchase $360.00 worth of items per month from the commissary. Family members and friends could send money to the commissary account through an intermediary in Iowa who processed all the funds for the BOP. Because many of the inmates had been in prison for a long time, and had little or no family contact, most of the inmates had to rely on other sources of income.

There is an interesting shadow economy within the BOP. It is, in large part, a barter system, based upon United States postage stamps and/or certain items purchased in the commissary. Packets of mackerel purchased from the commissary were commonly used for currency. When I was in Edgefield, the stamps had a value of $.45 each. In this next chapter, I will give a few specific details on how these funds were used to purchase a variety of items, most of which were considered contraband.

CHAPTER 8

A LOT OF JOBS ARE CREATED BY LOCKING PEO-
ple up. The government pays to lock people up and inmates do not
have the ability to collectively bargain. In most cases, they have
waived all their constitutional rights. According to an article in the
Wall Street Journal about private prisons, one company was willing
to pay the government over $190 million dollars to own and oper-
ate prison facilities if the government would guarantee a 90% occupancy rate for the next 20 years.

Imprisoning people has become one of America's high growth
businesses, in part, because inmates can help manufacture any number of items at such a low wage. Low wages, and long separation
from family and friends, forces inmates to seek alternative sources
of finance.

There are always inmates willing to perform tasks. They
will clean cubicles, iron shirts, do laundry, or clean tennis shoes.
Compensation for these legitimate tasks varied from 1 to 3 stamps.

Other inmates would sell food they stole from the kitchen.
Obviously, inmates working in the kitchen could realize all profit
from selling products they didn't have to pay for. A green pepper
and onion would sell for 3 to 4 stamps. An onion, green pepper and
tomato, called a "Mexican", would generally sell for six stamps. Why
would anyone want to buy these items?

The food prepared in the mess hall is terrible. I lost 35 pounds in the first six weeks. While some of the weight loss was attributable to a flu virus that was going around, much of it was because of the food. I recall having to cut off the top half of the breakfast cake because of the mouse droppings on top. It had been prepared the night before. As a result, many of the inmates prepared their own meals using the microwaves provided in the units. Pizzas, nachos with cheese, tomatoes and onion and Stromboli sandwiches are just a few of the things inmates prepared.

Several times each month, the guards would come through each unit and inspect every locker looking for contraband. Food items purchased were consumed as soon as possible. Having any food in your locker, other than what you could buy at the commissary, was prohibited.

The staff was sometimes lenient when it came to food items. They were primarily looking for cell phones, alcohol, cigarettes and drugs. Inmates caught with any of these items would be sent to the SHU, known as "the hole," for 4 to 6 weeks, depending on the items found. In some cases, they would be sent to another facility, based upon previous offenses.

You may be wondering how these items find their way into the facility.

Many items are brought in by the staff. Because these items can be sold for such a high price, the temptation is great.

Depending on availability, cigarettes generally sold for 8 to 10 stamps each. At 10 stamps, the prison cost of one cigarette would be $4.50. With 20 cigarettes in a pack, the value was $90.00. A carton of cigarettes would be valued at $900.00.

Buying a carton of cigarettes for $35-$50 and selling them to inmates for this exponential profit was tempting for staff.

While not all staff members were corrupt, many took advantage of the system. One staff member had a financial interest in a local restaurant. Much of the food meant for the inmates found its way to that restaurant. Eggs were on the menu but, in the nine months I was there, I never saw one served in the mess hall. They could be purchased, however, for a few stamps. I remember standing in line to use the phone when the person in front of me said I could go ahead of him if I had a hard-boiled egg. Unfortunately, I did not have one. When I told the person, I was calling this story, she thought I was kidding. I said, "You keep forgetting where I am." You can't make this stuff up. My first meal out was two over-easy eggs at the Waffle House.

After seeing the profit margin on cigarettes, you can only imagine what could be realized by selling other contraband like alcohol, drugs and cell phones.

Occupancy in my unit averaged 140 inmates. By my estimate, 60 had cell phones at any given time. It was an interesting game. Everyone knew the phones were coming in through the staff, but the guards were constantly trying to confiscate them. One night, a female guard was chasing an inmate with a cellphone through the unit. He locked himself in a bathroom stall and was trying to break up the phone and flush it down the toilet. The next day, the staff pulled the commode out of the floor in an attempt to find the phone. On another occasion, the same guard wrestled an inmate in his bed who was trying to swallow the sim card. He bit her on the finger and was sent next door to the hole. We never saw him again.

These were common, nightly, occurrences. When I went to use the restroom early one morning, there were two guys sitting on the floor drinking from a vodka bottle and smoking a joint.

CHAPTER 9

ONE INMATE, WHO HAD BEEN IN PRISON SINCE 1992, had still not completed his GED requirement. I jokingly suggested to the class instructor, another inmate teaching the class, that he should try using teaching examples to which the inmates could relate. Because no one seemed to have a problem calculating the costs associated with buying contraband, it should not be too difficult to come up with an analogy to assist in the learning process. The instructor said he had already tried that and told me the following example.

The instructor asked the students to assume that there were 30 people working in the kitchen. He asked them, "If 30% were caught stealing and sent to the hole, how many people would be left?" The closest answer he got was, "I don't know, but I'm sure there are more than 30% stealing!!!"

I spent my time at Edgefield walking several miles a day and reading a lot of books. The library was small and limited, but I could order books from the outside library. There were a few pieces of exercise equipment located in a very small room. There was a wall to play handball, a softball field, and a basketball court.

There were also 2 bocce ball courts. Inmates improvised weightlifting by filling pillowcases with sand and putting them in plastic milk cartons. The steel bars used for this weightlifting were buried every evening in the sand of the volleyball area. Everyone knew they were there, but it was overlooked.

We were allowed visitors every two weeks. The visitation room was very small and always overcrowded. Often, we were forced to sit with other families. On more than one occasion, I witnessed guards turning certain family members away, including children, because of the dress code. This perceived "dress code" seemed to apply mostly to the white visitors. Some were turned away for wearing designer jeans. Many people had traveled great distances and were forced to change clothes in their car or buy other clothing locally.

When visitation was over, we were required to strip down to be inspected for contraband. Once again, we opened our mouths, spread our buttock cheeks, lifted our testicles, and had the bottoms of our feet inspected. Humiliation and degradation seemed to be the main goal. On one occasion, an inmate lost visitation privileges for a month because he waved to his family getting into their car in the parking lot. They said he had made inappropriate contact with someone outside the prison facility.

The medical and dental health policy in the BOP is designed to provide only necessary treatments for the greatest number of inmates with available resources. This is the nice way of stating that the BOP does not encourage healthcare issues. The saying among inmates is, "Stay healthy. If you get sick, you die." Medical emergencies were treated on Tuesdays.

I had lost so much weight (35 pounds in six weeks), my wedding ring kept slipping off my finger. Once, when I tried to grab it before it hit the floor, I sliced my finger open on the top corner of my metal locker. It was bleeding pretty badly, and I thought it might require stitches. I wrapped it tightly in some toilet paper and walked down to the medical office. I asked the nurse if she would look at my finger. She told me to keep pressure on it and wash it with soap and water. I asked if I could get a band-aid. She held up her hands and said, "We don't give those out."

Each night, there is a "call out" sheet posted on a bulletin board and everyone is responsible for checking to see if they have any "callouts" for the following day. Shortly after I arrived at Edgefield, I was told to report to medical for a physical exam at noon the following day.

I reported as instructed. There were two other inmates there from other units. The medical door was locked, so we waited outside for 45 minutes. Finally, I asked one of the guards passing by if he knew when the medical department would open. He had a key and went in to see if anyone was in the office. He came back and reported that no one was in. I told him we had been waiting for more than an hour and asked him what we should do. He told us to go back to our units and wait for them to page us to come back. Approximately 3 hours later, I heard my name paged to report to medical. The other two inmates who had reported with me earlier had been paged as well. We saw the compound doctor who was supposed to give the physicals. I do not know where this guy went to medical school, but the physical was a joke. He took my blood pressure and told me to extend my arms and touch my nose. He asked if I wanted a prostate exam. I found out later that this was his standard question of all inmates. I declined that procedure and was told to report back to my unit.

That evening, around 8 PM, I was paged to report to the administrative office. When I arrived, the other two inmates who had reported to medical with me were also there. The guard opened the front door and told all three of us to get in the car because we were being taken next door to the federal penitentiary. We were concerned and very nervous. I asked why we were being taken next door.

He said, "I'm not telling you again. Get in the car. They will tell you when you get next door." Once there, we were told to wait in the lobby until the lieutenant showed up.

A few minutes later, the lieutenant came in and said we were all being written up for not reporting to the medical office on time. He said we were supposed to be there at 1 PM but did not show up, and that we had to be paged several times before we finally showed up around 5 PM. As a result, we were all being given a written reprimand, and the points would go against our record for good behavior. He asked if anyone had anything to say.

I told him that I had quite a bit to say. Even though I did not know the other two inmates from different units, I told him that they had reported with me at noon, as we had been instructed. I suggested someone check the "call out sheet" to confirm the correct time. We were instructed to report at noon, not one.

I told him that, when we arrived, the door was locked and that this could be confirmed with the guard who told us no one was in the medical office.

Fortunately, I remembered the guard's name. I told him that all three of us reported back at 5 PM, which was the first time we had been paged. He said that, if that was the case, he could not write us up, and that he would check my story with the guard the next day. We got back in the car and were driven back to our units next door.

About an hour later, we were paged once again to go to the administrative office. We were told to get back in the car and were driven next door again. When we went in, the lieutenant handed each of us a written reprimand. He said he would tear them up the next day if the guard confirmed my story. We were driven back. Apparently, he never filed the reprimands because they were never in my file and nothing else was ever said.

The lazy doctor did not show up at his scheduled time to conduct the exams.

He thought he could cover that up by blaming the three of us, so he reported that we did not report as instructed. I found out later that this was a common practice for this doctor. This guy was so stupid he did not even cite the correct time in his complaint against us to the lieutenant. Welcome to BOP healthcare.

Before we leave Edgefield, we should cover what's called "diesel therapy." Diesel therapy is the term used when inmates are required to travel. This process occurred many times during my stay at Edgefield.

On one occasion, an inmate, who had self-surrendered to the facility, was required to appear in court in Atlanta. He was an engineer who had worked with government contracts and, apparently, accepted some vacation kickbacks for his work. It was a white-collar crime and he had no previous criminal record.

The drive from Edgefield to Atlanta takes approximately 3 hours. The inmate had self-surrendered and posed no threat of escape. The most cost-efficient way for him to make his court appearance would be to grant him a leave of absence for the one or two days required for his court appearance. His hearing date was scheduled for some time in November. He was told in June that he would be leaving for his court appearance. He was taken to the penitentiary facility next door for processing. He was handcuffed and shackled with several other inmates, many of whom were from the penitentiary. They were loaded onto a bus and began their long and arduous journey. During the next 5 ½ months he was forced to spend the night in several different county jails. He was locked up 23 hours each day. For the other hour each day, he had a choice of going outside to a walking area, taking a shower, or making a phone call.

During this journey, he was flown on "Con Air" to Puerto Rico and to Oklahoma. I think he may have even gone to California. One can only imagine the cost. This is not an exception. You would be shocked to know the frequency with which this happens. He could have made his court appearance with a three-hour car ride, accompanied by federal marshals, more humanely and at considerably less expense.

When this inmate returned to the facility 5 ½ months later, I did not recognize him. He had lost over 50 pounds and looked like he had just come from Auschwitz.

CHAPTER 10

————

I SPENT A TOTAL OF NINE MONTHS AT EDGEFIELD. On November 14, 2012, I was released from Edgefield, issued a BOP photo ID, and instructed to report to the Residential Reentry Center in Fort Myers, Florida. The Center was a part of the Salvation Army. The town driver, another inmate, drove me to the airport in Augusta where I caught a connecting flight to Atlanta, then on to Fort Myers. My wife met me at the airport and drove me to the Residential Reentry Center. I was instructed to report there by 9 PM. We arrived around 8:30 PM.

Once there, another photo ID was taken, and I was assigned a room. There were four people, including me, in the room. It had a sink, and we shared a toilet and shower with four other people in the adjoining room. I was given a breathalyzer and required to submit to a urinalysis. I now had two photo IDs that had been issued by the BOP.

The following week, I needed a legal document notarized. When I presented my photo IDs to the Notary who worked at the facility she said, "I can't accept these. I need to see your driver's license." I said, "I don't understand." My photo ID had been issued at the facility. Her comment was, "Anybody can make these up. I need to see your driver's license." Still confused I said, "Do you think I have someone else doing my time for me?" She said she could not notarize any document without seeing my driver's license. You can only imagine the problems I encountered in getting a new driver's license with only a BOP photo ID. I finally got one. Welcome to Residential Reentry.

Residents were required to seek employment and pay 25% of their gross income for food and housing. Because I was eligible for home confinement in December, and my release date from the BOP was December 28, 2012, I was not required to seek employment. For the few weeks I resided at the halfway house, I could go to various doctor and dental appointments. My wife could pick me up and take me to each of the appointments. While at the facility, I was required to take 11 or 12 hours of residential reentry classes. Many times, the instructors never showed up and we watched a movie.

When I was finally released to home confinement, I was required to wear a GPS tracking monitor. Even though I was wearing a monitor, they would call me at one or two o'clock every morning to verify I was there. On several random occasions, I was called to report back to the facility for a breathalyzer and urinalysis test. It did not matter that the judge had excused me from any mandatory drug or alcohol testing.

It appears to me that system is designed to perpetuate itself. The cost inefficiencies are too numerous to mention. While on home confinement, I was required to report to the facility once per week. Once I showed up, I could leave.

Finally, home confinement ended. We were looking forward to rebuilding our lives. We have no children. We had a small 4 lbs. 6 oz. Maltese dog, who meant everything to us. We thought the worst was behind us. We were wrong.

CHAPTER 11

———

If we had no winter, the spring would not be so pleasant;

If we did not sometimes taste adversity, Prosperity would not be so welcome.

— Anne Bradstreet

TWO DAYS BEFORE I HAD TO REPORT TO FEDERAL prison, I received at 258-page civil lawsuit from one of Capitol's investors. The lawsuit tried to tie me to the Capitol Ponzi scheme. The plaintiff sued me for several million dollars he had lost in Capitol. This creditor had been a friend and longtime real estate investor. When I called him to ask what was going on, he said he was unaware that a lawsuit had been filed. He said his lawyers told him that he needed to "stay in the loop."

This investor is exceptionally wealthy. He had given more money to charity than he lost with his Capitol investment. It became obvious that he had delegated everything to his lawyers. Because of his wealth, they had an unlimited budget to pursue actions against me. Their self-serving interests were immediately apparent. The strategy seemed to be vitriolic persistence.

In 2010, the bankruptcy trustee for Capitol Investments sued me personally for over $115 million.

In August 2010, another investor who lost money in Capitol filed a "Motion for Break Order." The motion requested an order authorizing the sheriff to enter our home, day or night, by whatever means necessary, to seize all my personal property. The personal property listed to be seized included my toothbrush, socks, comb, razor, clothes, and underwear. The motion was frightening in its scope and content. We were genuinely concerned for our safety and that of our small dog.

Upon the advice of counsel, in September 2010, I filed a Chapter 11 voluntary bankruptcy petition. We were advised that this would put a temporary hold on the Motion for Break Order and that a bankruptcy trustee would be assigned to mitigate the issues.

The Department of Justice believes it is important to keep the victims of a federal crime informed of court proceedings. Through the Victim Notification System(VNS), individuals affected are provided with updated scheduling and event information as the case proceeds through the criminal justice system.

On October 11, 2011, a notice was sent from the United States Attorney's office in New Jersey to all victims of Capitol Investments. It stated, "Earlier this month, you received a letter regarding filed charges against Sydney Jack Williams. The lead prosecutor for this case is Jacob Elberg. The letter sent earlier this month mistakenly stated that the main charge Sydney Jack Williams pleaded guilty to is characterized as securities fraud. In fact, Sydney Jack Williams pleaded guilty to filing a false income tax return. The government Does Not Allege that Sydney Jack Williams was aware that Nevin Shapiro or Capitol Investments USA, Inc. were engaged in fraud."

I had been investigated by the FBI, SEC and IRS. They had concluded that I was a victim of the Ponzi scheme, as opposed to being culpable for it. It did not stop some people from suing me.

CHAPTER 12

———

WHEN I FILED FOR CHAPTER 11 BANKRUPTCY IN September 2010, a bankruptcy trustee was assigned to my case. This was the first of three bankruptcy trustees I ultimately encountered. The break order that had been filed and the fear we were experiencing was my sole motivation for filing. I had engaged a local bankruptcy attorney to assist me in the process.

Hindsight is 20/20. Had I known then what I know today, I would never have filed for bankruptcy. Because of all my former interests in real estate investments throughout the country, the documentation I needed to gather, and the paperwork I needed to complete, was overwhelming and complicated. My attorney told me I had to undergo credit counseling from an approved credit counseling agency which I could do mostly online, before the filing could become official. Everyone had their hand out for a fee.

The United States Trustee Program is the component of the Department of Justice that works to protect the integrity of the bankruptcy system by overseeing case administration and litigating to enforce the bankruptcy laws.

Generally, the duties of the US trustee in a Chapter 11 bankruptcy case are set forth in 28 U.S.C section 586." They include:

- First day orders

- Official committees

- Reorganization plans, disclosure statements

- Ensuring compliance

- Preventing delay

- Professional employment

- Fraud

Courts are required to charge $1167.00 as a case filing fee, and a $550.00 miscellaneous administrative fee.

I was required to open a debtor-in-possession checking account and submit monthly income and expense operating reports. This was especially cumbersome because of the multiplicity of real estate holdings. All income I received was to be deposited into the debtor-in-possession checking account. This account, while being monitored monthly, was to be used to pay my monthly expenses, including home mortgage payments, health insurance, food, and general living expenses.

Shortly after I opened the account, the bankruptcy trustee filed a motion with the court requesting that she be given sole authority over my debtor-in-possession account. That request was granted by the court.

Shortly after being given sole control over the account, the trustee stopped paying all my living expenses. Instead, the funds were used to pay the trustee, and other miscellaneous administrative expenses. These were approved by the court.

The US trustee was required to conduct "341 hearings". Under oath, I was required to answer all the trustee's questions and any questions from creditors who attended. The hearings were held each month. After each hearing, I had until the next hearing to bring any additional requested information. During the next 11 months, I provided all the information requested. This included my personal tax returns as well as tax returns on all real estate entities. Eleven (11) months of 341 hearings is unprecedented. No stone was left unturned.

During most of the 341 hearings, I received little support from my attorney. He did not show up at my first 341 hearing. Instead, he sent an associate who was not at all familiar with my case.

I was often left on my own to complete and provide the requested information, which was complicated and confusing. More often than not, when I had a question, my attorney handed me off to his administrative assistant. She tried to be as helpful as she could in completing all the necessary paperwork and filings. Many times, I asked my criminal defense attorney if he thought I had completed everything accurately in the bankruptcy. While he helped as best he could, he was not a bankruptcy attorney. He had difficulty getting my bankruptcy attorney to return his calls.

As one example, which may seem insignificant, I was asked if I owned or had a safe deposit box. I did not have a safe deposit box. My wife had one, but she was not filing for bankruptcy. The Chapter 11 form did not ask about a spouse's safe deposit box. That question was asked only for those filing a Chapter 7 or Chapter 13 bankruptcy application. Regardless, I did disclose that my wife had a safe deposit box, that contained only her personal effects. Nothing in the safe deposit box was mine.

Five years later, I was indicted for bankruptcy fraud over the safe deposit box.

CHAPTER 13

———

WE RECEIVED AN IRS TAX REFUND IN DECEMBER 2009. Because of all the civil litigation I was encountering, my criminal defense attorney was concerned that some creditor or creditors would be able to freeze my wife's checking account even though she was not a party to any of the litigation. I asked how that could be possible. He said he had heard of cases where this had happened, and it was a concern. I asked how we would pay our bills if that happened. He responded that "they didn't care," and that sometimes accounts could be tied up for years while "they sorted everything out."

Confronted with this frightening scenario, I asked if my wife should start to withdraw some cash for a reserve so that we could pay our bills. He said he saw no problem with that. The money was obviously from a legitimate source: The United States government. The money from the tax refund had been deposited in a legitimate checking account. It was being withdrawn for the legitimate purpose of paying bills.

I had a good relationship with the bank. My office was in the same building and I maintained many real estate accounts with it. The bank suggested that each cash withdrawal be for less than $10,000, for security purposes when leaving the bank.

Because of all the litigation, my wife and I were reluctant to do anything without the approval of our attorney. With his blessing, in

March and April 2010, my wife wrote a total of 35 checks payable to cash. She put the cash in our home safe. On 12 of those occasions, she gave me her check and I brought the funds home to her. Even though all the withdrawals were in an amount less than $10,000, it was a small bank and they had to make arrangements to have even that much cash available every day.

The withdrawals were made in March and April 2010. I did not file for Chapter 11 bankruptcy protection until September 2010. During the 11 months of 341 hearings, I disclosed that the cash withdrawals had been made. In addition to notifying all creditors of the withdrawals, I also notified the IRS and Justice Department of the cash withdrawals when I filed my financial disclosure form in New Jersey in 2011.

Almost 5 years later, I was indicted, along with my wife, for a crime called "structuring."

CHAPTER 14

━━━━━

AN INVOLUNTARY BANKRUPTCY IS COMMENCED
when one or more creditors files a petition with the bankruptcy
court. Once the petition is filed, the debtor has 20 days to respond
to the petition. If the debtor does not respond, the court will allow
the bankruptcy and the debtor will have no choice but to participate.
Capitol Investments was forced into involuntary bankruptcy by the
group of Chicago Real estate investors who had lost money.

During the course of my Chapter 11 voluntary bankruptcy,
the Capitol Investments trustee was appointed. The trustee was to
be reimbursed for his time on an hourly basis. The trustee's charter
was to determine if there were any recoverable assets that could be
liquidated for the benefit of creditors. Because Capitol had done little
legitimate business after 2005, it was determined early on that there
were few, if any, assets that could be recovered.

Nearly all of Capitol's transactions involved promissory notes
with each investor. My first investment with Capitol was in the form
of a promissory note that was personally guaranteed by Capitol and
Shapiro. The note was payable at 10% per annum, but the interest
was paid, and principal was returned at the end of 30 days.

Most of Capitol's transactions with investors were structured
the same way. All the investments were short-term. Generally, the
interest was paid, and the capital was returned within 30 to 60 days.

The trustee took the position that the structure of those loans to Capitol were in violation of Florida's usury interest rate law. Usury laws limit the amount of interest that can be charged on a loan. These laws are designed to protect consumers.

Florida currently has a maximum interest rate of 18%.

The Capitol trustee took the position that I should have received only $4,166.66 interest on a $500,000 loan. No reasonable business person would risk half a million dollars for a $4,166.66 return. Because the loan was repaid within 30 days, the trustee took the position that it was a 120% annualized return, rather than a 10% fee. All the investor loans to Capitol were in this category.

The Capitol trustee saw an opportunity to pursue investors who lost money under his usurer's interest rate theory. Even though the investor may have been a net loser, the trustee threatened legal action for receiving a criminally usury interest rate. Confronted with this frightening scenario, investors were more than willing to reach a settlement agreement with the trustee.

The trustee recognized an opportunity to claw back funds from investors, while being exponentially compensated by taking a percentage of the funds rather than an hourly rate. The trustee petitioned the court to receive 33 1/3% of all monies recovered. The court granted the trustee's request.

The investors who lost money became the victims again. The trustee sued me for $115 million dollars. He used the ridiculous theory that the $500,000 I originally invested was really $6 million dollars because the same funds were repaid and reinvested monthly for 12 months. Once the trustee determined that I had virtually no recoverable assets, I settled with the trustee for approximately $33,000 that I obtained from the sale of our home.

CHAPTER 15

THE HITS KEPT COMING. MY CHAPTER 11 TRUSTEE stopped paying our bills. All available funds went to pay her fees and trustee expenses. My wife used her own funds to pay our ongoing expenses. The Chapter 11 trustee sent my wife a bill for $27,000 for "overseeing" my wife's payment of our bills. She called it an "administrative fee".

The bankruptcy trustee for Capitol and for my bankruptcy would soon be outdone by a third trustee.

My home was owned by a private annuity trust (PAT). PAT is a legal arrangement used with highly appreciated assets, such as real estate or an investment portfolio.

PATs were used to defer federal capital gains tax on the sale of an asset, to provide a stream of income, and to remove the assets from the owner's estate, thus reducing or eliminating the estate taxes.

Prior to October 2006, PAT's allowed the owner of an investment property to defer up to 100% of the taxes without ever having to buy another property. This is very important because good quality investment properties are difficult to locate. The PAT also allowed the seller of a highly appreciated primary residence to defer up to 100 % of the taxes. This is important because all gains on primary residences over $250,000 for a single person, and $500,000 for a married couple are taxed, if a PAT is not used. Under a PAT, the original owner of the asset pays taxes on future PAT payments received, not on the transfer of the asset to the PAT.

I established a PAT on December 27, 2004, and another on March 15, 2006.

On March 24, 2006, the 2006 PAT entered into a land contract with an unrelated party to sell my primary residence. The purchase price was $3,500,000. $500,000 was paid upon execution and delivery of the land contract.

The remaining unpaid principal balance was to be paid in installments together with an interest rate of 7% per annum. There were no prepayment penalties or restrictions. All financing conditions were being met and the purchaser obtained a conventional 80% mortgage financing commitment.

Once the conditions of the land contract had been met, a Warranty Deed was issued on March 27, 2007, and the property was transferred to the purchaser.

In February 2010, a bankruptcy trustee was appointed in Ohio, over my former home and purchaser's business. In March 2011, the purchaser of my former residence was arrested and charged. The Ohio bankruptcy trustee seized my former home.

In May 2012, the Ohio trustee allowed the property to be sold, and title was transferred to a third person for good and valuable consideration.

On August 28, 2014, one day before the statute of limitations expired, the Ohio trustee sued my PAT for approximately $760,000. The 20% down payment that the purchaser paid for my house in 2006 he had borrowed from his company. The trustee alleged that my PAT was a fraudulent transfer from the purchaser's company.

The Ohio trustee was seeking to retain both the full value of the property which he allowed to be sold in 2012, and $760,000 of the purchase price paid to acquire it.

My PAT had sold my home to an unrelated party, just as millions of homes are sold every day. It entered into a sales contract. The buyer wired their 20% down payment to the title company handling the closing. The buyer got a traditional lender to finance the 80%

balance. Once all the funds were in escrow with the title company, a warranty deed was issued for good and valuable consideration. The PAT which owned the home received the purchaser's monies from the title company. Title was transferred to the new owners.

Five years later, the purchaser of the home was indicted in a different state. My PAT was sued because the purchaser had borrowed the 20% down payment from his company.

The Ohio trustee sued all the beneficiaries of the PAT, including my father who had passed away in 2005. The Ohio trustee alleged that the PAT was the "alter ego" of not only myself but my wife. It did not matter that the statute of limitations for suing her had expired over a year earlier. This was clearly a pay-me-to-go- away lawsuit.

CHAPTER 16

———

OUR JOURNEY THROUGH CIVIL, CRIMINAL, AND bankruptcy litigation had become quite costly. We no longer had the resources to fight the Ohio trustee litigation. The PAT had hired three different legal firms specializing in bankruptcy to defend the claims.

From the very beginning of this lawsuit, I wanted to have a summary judgment filed on the merits of the claim. Instead, the firms hired by the PAT filed esoteric motions to dismiss based on technical grounds that had nothing to do with the merits of the claim. A great deal of time was expended in multiple depositions and requests for documents that were entirely irrelevant to the merits of the action against the PAT. The bulk of that discovery was devoted to the Ohio trustee's search for assets owned by the PAT, or by others, from which he might seek to collect a judgment in his favor against the PAT, if he ever got one.

In addition, a great deal of time and effort was wasted by lawyers arguing over which trust records had been properly requested or which records were "relevant" to the issues of the lawsuit. The court ultimately ordered all the trust records produced, without redaction or limitation. Binder after binder of records were produced. In fact, only two documents were relevant: the 2006 PAT document and the home purchase contract. None of this did anything to advance the resolution of the case or the Ohio trustee's claim against the trust.

The PAT's attorneys did not initiate any discovery until February 23, 2015.

The Ohio trustee knew he would lose this case on summary judgment if any of the attorneys representing the trust would ever file one. This was a nuisance lawsuit designed for the sole purpose of having someone pay something for it go away.

The assets of the PAT were depleted. A total of approximately $500,000 was incurred in legal fees in defending the simple sale of a house. This cost was five times the value of the PAT. I was told the Ohio trustee had billed expenses in excess of $400,000.

CHAPTER 17

---

*When we long for life without difficulties, remind us
that oaks grow strong in contrary winds and diamonds
are made under pressure.*

— Peter Marshall

BECAUSE THE PAT NO LONGER HAD THE ASSETS
to continue funding the legal expenses, the PAT entered into a settlement agreement. The PAT's lawyer agreed to accept the maximum possible judgment against the PAT, without requiring the
Ohio trustee to prove he had any claim against the PAT at all. All
the assets of the trust were thrown away, with no substantive defense
having ever been asserted. The Ohio trustee was now able to pursue his "alter ego" claims against my wife and myself to collect his
agreed judgement.

We were now forced to represent ourselves "pro se" in this litigation. "Pro se" is a Latin phrase that means "through itself." It also
means "YOU'RE SCREWED". We were now representing ourselves.

The Ohio bankruptcy court allocated two days for the issues
to be litigated. My wife and I were now forced to review over 10,000
pages of documents in just a few weeks, and to appear in Ohio

federal court to defend ourselves against the Ohio Trustee's battery of lawyers.

Everybody involved in the home sale was a Florida resident. The PAT were Florida entities. The asset sold was a Florida home. We had no connection to the state of Ohio that would explain why we were subject to the exercise of personal jurisdiction or venue against us in Ohio.

From the very beginning, we thanked the Ohio court in advance for its patience and understanding in allowing us to present the facts of the case ourselves. It was not our intent to argue points of law, as we were not qualified to do so.

The Ohio trustee lawyers purposely tried to prejudice the court by associating me with the Capitol Investments Ponzi scheme in Miami, as well as the "structuring" issue we were facing in Fort Myers. Neither the Ohio trustee nor the Ohio court had any knowledge of the actual facts and circumstances surrounding either of those issues.

The Ohio trustee allowed the purchaser to sell the house in 2012, presumably to benefit the creditors the Ohio trustee was representing. Because the Ohio trustee waited almost 2 ½ years to sell the home, it was now too late to take any steps to retrieve the home or to make a claim against the title insurance company. The Ohio trustee was now trying to realize the full value of the property by the sale, as well as recover back the down payment used to acquire the home.

Under the Ohio trustee's bizarre legal theory, no one would be able to sell anything. Anytime someone sold a home, they would have to do a forensic audit of screening the purchasers down payment. They would need to be clairvoyant so that they could see years into the future.

How would anyone be expected to know where a purchaser's down payment came from? The down payment wired was booked as a loan from the purchaser's company. He may have deposited his personal funds or his company paycheck into that account. His company may have made a payment as a distribution to him or for a payment of a pre-existing debt owed to him by his company. A wire transfer from a company account does not imply that the funds in the account were being stolen by the company's CEO.

After several trips from Florida to Ohio, I tried the case myself.

The court found in our favor. The court recommended that the district court enter judgment for us because Florida law did not recognize the cause of action asserted by the trustee. The Ohio trustee filed a 26-page objection to the ruling, but the District Court upheld the court's decision.

We won the battle, but we lost the war. All the PAT's assets had been depleted defending this nuisance lawsuit in another state in the middle of the country.

CHAPTER 18

———

It is easier to live through someone else than to complete yourself.

The freedom to lead and plan your own life is frightening if you have never faced it before.

It is frightening when a person finally realizes that there is no answer to the question" who am I" except the voice inside.

—Betty Friedan

MULTIPLE CREDITORS WERE NOW SMELLING blood. No one seemed willing to accept responsibility for the decisions they made. While dealing with the Ohio trustee lawsuit, we were also dealing with ongoing civil litigation in Florida as well as the criminal "structuring" allegation.

This is a picture of what life was like for Lorie and me following the collapse of Capitol Investments. It was against this backdrop that Lorie made the cash withdrawals mentioned earlier. We were notified in March 2013, that we were both being indicted for bankruptcy fraud and "structuring."

CHAPTER 19

———

AFTER I WAS NOTIFIED OF THESE ALLEGATIONS in March 2013, I met with my criminal defense attorney to find out what he was talking about. "What bankruptcy fraud are they alleging and what is "'structuring?'"

My criminal attorney had never heard of "structuring." I'll bet you haven't either. He hired an outside consultant to research the structuring statute and how it could possibly apply to our situation. We discovered that my Chapter 11 bankruptcy trustee had notified the assistant US attorney of a possible "structuring" violation after my 341 hearings.

"Structuring "is conducting cash transactions with a bank with the intent of avoiding the banks obligation to report suspicious cash transactions to the government.

The intent of the "structuring" statute was to discover people trying to hide monies illegally obtained or funds being used for an illegal purpose. It was never intended to apply to people withdraw-ing lawfully obtained funds from their own checking account to pay for legitimate expenses. Unfortunately, the statute is so poorly writ-ten that it is open to interpretations far outside its purpose.

As far as the bankruptcy fraud is concerned, they were alleging that I failed to disclose that I had theoretical access to my wife's safe deposit box. Apparently, it did not matter that I had disclosed my wife's safe deposit box during my 341 hearings, or that its contents we're solely hers.

My wife's safe deposit box had been disclosed. The fact that the cash had been withdrawn from her account had been disclosed to the US Department of Justice and IRS in New Jersey when I completed my financial disclosure form in 2011. The cash withdrawals were disclosed to all creditors during my 341 hearings.

CHAPTER 20

Everything we see is a perspective, not the truth.

— Marcus Aurelius

ROBERT W WOOD, A FORBES CONTRIBUTOR, recently wrote an article stating that 91% of the IRS seizures for "structuring" involve lawful taxpayers.

The Bank Secrecy Act requires financial institutions to report currency transactions in excess of $10,000 to the IRS. The "structuring" law makes it a crime to structure currency transactions to avoid the reports. All our withdrawals were in an amount less than $10,000. The funds came from a tax refund received from the US Treasury. The government's position was that we structured transactions under $10,000 to avoid the bank reporting it to the agency it came from.

The IRS criminal investigation division enforces the rules on cash transactions. A new report from the treasury inspector general for tax administration (TIGTA), says the law is enforced primarily against individuals and businesses whose income was legally obtained. The report says the rights of some individuals and businesses were compromised in these investigations. No kidding.

If a taxpayer is structuring transactions to avoid the reports, the structured amounts are subject to civil forfeiture proceedings. The US constitution requires that penalties in civil forfeiture cases be proportionate to the conduct resulting in the forfeiture. Squaring these rules has been controversial.

There have been complaints about seizures of property without sufficient evidence of a crime for a long time.

TIGTA audited to determine how seizures and forfeitures are conducted, what procedures the IRS uses, and whether those procedures are fair. The report isn't rosy. It found that in 91% of the 278 investigations sampled where the source of funds could be determined, the funds were obtained legally.

The overall purpose of the IRS civil forfeiture program is to disrupt and dismantle criminal enterprises, not legal ones. Most people impacted were not involved in criminal enterprises or engaged in illegal activity.

They were running legal businesses like jewelry stores, restaurants, and gas stations.

According to the report, the government pursued the cases where the source of the funds was legal because the Department of Justice had encouraged task forces to engage in "quick hits." Property can be seized more quickly, and the matter can be more quickly resolved through negotiation, if the source of the funds is legal instead of the result of criminal activity (such as drug trafficking and money laundering). Real criminal cases are more time-consuming and expensive. The government instead opted for the "quick hits". The report suggests that investigating crime did not seem to be a high priority.

In most cases, the government relied on the pattern of currency transactions to support the seizure, rather than interviewing the property owners. When property owners were interviewed after the seizure, agents did not identify themselves properly, explain the purpose of the interviews, or advise property owners of any rights they might have. At the conclusion of the interviews, they told the property owners they had committed a crime.

In 54 cases, property owners gave reasonable explanations for why their currency transactions did not exceed $10,000. In most cases, TIGTA found no evidence that the government bothered to investigate these explanations. The government routinely promised non-prosecution in exchange for the civil forfeiture. In 2014, the government changed its policy so that it would only pursue illegal source income structuring cases unless there are "exceptional circumstances." In 2016, after two congressional hearings, criminal investigators began notifying approximately 1800 property owners who had forfeited funds that they could petition for return of their funds.

TIGTA made recommendations for improvement. "This report reaffirms our committee's findings that the government has repeatedly and knowingly abused its authority to wrongly target and seize money from hard working Americans," said House Ways and Means Committee Chairman Kevin Brady R-Texas, Tax Policy Subcommittee Chairman Peter Roskam, R-Illinois, and Oversight Subcommittee Chairman, Vern Buchanan,R- Florida, in a joint statement.

I believe that, because of my prior conviction for subscribing to an inaccurate tax return, we had been identified as a "quick hit" target. It did not matter that the "structured" funds did not come from an illegal source or go to an illegal recipient. It did not matter that the they were not used for any illegal purpose. If Lorie's withdrawals had been for exactly $10,000, there would have been no crime at all.

We were now the victims of "policing for profits". It is legal stealing by the government. It belongs in a nightmare dictatorship, not in a nation which supposedly prides itself on its system of justice.

Radley Balko wrote an article published in the Washington Post on March 24, 2014, stating that federal "structuring" laws are "smurfing" ridiculous. He said that it seems appropriate that the crime of structuring is also sometimes called "smurfing." "Structuring" is the act of breaking up financial transactions to get around the reporting requirements that kick in for transactions over a specific amount of money. The alternative term "smurfing" is a reference to the children's cartoon in which a large entity (the Smurf Village) is made up of several smaller ones (the Smurfs themselves).

If you grew up on the cartoon in the 1980s or were unfortunate enough to have seen the 2011 movie, you know that the word "Smurf" itself is ambiguous. It can mean whatever the person using the word wants it to mean. That is a pretty decent metaphor for a statute open to boundless interpretation in the hands of federal officials.

CHAPTER 21

IN 2015, AMERICANS LOST MORE THAN $5 BILLION to government and police aggression through civil asset forfeitures.

This is more than all the money stolen that year by burglars.

The Bank Secrecy Act requires banks to report to the federal government any activity from customers that might be construed as structuring deposits or withdrawals to avoid the reporting requirement.

The banks are prohibited from telling you that it has reported you to the government. Banks that fail to sufficiently police their customers, and banks that notify customers that they have been reported for suspicious activity, risk financial sanctions. Bank personnel found to have neglected their duties to report suspicious behavior can be criminally charged and sent to prison. As a result, there is quite a lot of incentive for banks to define "suspicious activity" broadly. There is a lot of risk for a bank in under-policing for structuring. There is no risk of losing customers for over-reporting them to the government. Most customers will never know.

The problem, of course, is that when banks are forced to cast such a wide net, they are going to report a lot of people who have done nothing wrong. In our case, we found ourselves in legal trouble. We were victims of an overzealous prosecution for a technical violation of a criminal regulatory statute of which we were not aware.

Years of civil and bankruptcy litigation had taken a tremendous financial toll. We were now confronted with criminal prosecution. We had to hire separate criminal defense attorneys for each of us. We were told that one lawyer could not represent both of us because of a potential conflict of interest. We were fortunate to have friends who loaned us money to cover legal expenses, even though we had no means to pay them back.

You never truly know yourself, or the strength of your friendships, until both are tested by adversity.

CHAPTER 22

———

MY PREVIOUS CRIMINAL DEFENSE ATTORNEY recommended that we retain other legal counsel so that he could be called as a witness. After all, he was the one who recommended that we accumulate a cash reserve and saw no problem with the cash withdrawals in 2010.

He recommended that we meet with two attorneys with whom he had worked in Miami. It was decided that, collectively, they could represent us both. They came to Naples, where we met in my previous attorney's office.

During the course of our many discussions, our Miami attorneys took little initiative in understanding the chronology of events that took place. The Miami attorneys were hesitant to even get the transcripts from my 341 hearings where I made all the disclosures. They kept telling me that it was not a level playing field or that they were correct.

Lorie and I both asked to take lie detector tests to confirm that we had no knowledge that withdrawing legal monies from our own checking account was a federal crime. We were told that lie detector results were not admissible in court.

Nevertheless, we were told that we could submit the results to the US Attorney.

We both took lie detector tests. The tests confirmed that it was never our intent to avoid a bank reporting requirement.

The purpose of a "mens rea" (Latin for "guilty mind") requirement is to require prosecutors to prove that a defendant acted with some degree of mental culpability. It prevents everyday Americans from becoming accidental criminals by doing something no reasonable person would know was wrong. Regrettably, in recent years congress and federal agencies have eliminated mens rea requirements, in creating thousands of crimes that require no proof of criminal intent, or are unclear as to what level of intent, if any, is necessary.

Senator Orin Hatch of Utah has long been a proponent of "mens rea" reform.

He has promoted legislation that would help protect individuals from being criminally prosecuted for accidental conduct or for doing something that should not be a crime in the first place. He has been largely unsuccessful.

Faced with this frightening reality, we became concerned that our defense attorneys could do little.

We paid $50,000 for what we thought would be a sound legal defense strategy. What we received was a five-page single spaced typed guilty plea agreement, frightening in its scope and content. The "structuring" sentencing guidelines included a $250,000 fine with a maximum of five years' imprisonment.

When we realized that this is all we could expect from our attorneys, we terminated their employment. We were unwilling to accept this alternative when we both knew we had done nothing intentionally wrong.

I retained another attorney from Miami, and Lorie retained an attorney in Fort Myers.

CHAPTER 23

The man who finds a wife finds a good thing, she is a blessing to him from the Lord.

Proverbs 18: 22 TLB

IT IS DIFFICULT TO PUT INTO WORDS ALL OUR thoughts and feelings at this time. It was hard to imagine that, after all that we had been through, beginning in 2009, up to and including our forced separation in 2012, we were now faced with another crisis. We had thought the worst was behind us. It wasn't.

Lorie had no reason to anticipate any of these events. We had lived a highly successful lifestyle until the beginning of 2009. Life had changed dramatically after the collapse of Capitol Investments. While the material losses were enormous, the emotional ones for Lorie were more devastating. Most of her friends turned against her. As one friend told her, others simply decided that it was not fun to have a relationship with someone who was no longer wealthy.

When I reported to Edgefield, Lorie found herself alone. She was forced to move out of her home. She had no support group. Her mother was in the Midwest and her remaining friends lived out-of-state.

Despite everything, Lorie never wavered. She continued to provide emotional support during my incarceration. I received daily letters, sometimes several in the same day. She visited every few weeks. We tried to talk twice a day. There was not one occasion, during the entire nine months, when she did not immediately answer my call.

It was unfathomable that we were once again caught up in the system, only this time both of us were confronted with criminal allegations and potentially forced separation.

CHAPTER 24

Problems are not stop signs, they are guideposts.

— Robert H Schuller

WITHOUT A STRONG SPIRITUAL FOUNDATION, we could never have survived, or overcome, these obstacles.

On March 29, 2015, Lorie felt a calling to be more involved in the church. She attended Living Waters Church in our community for the first time. She felt comfortable and enjoyed the service. She asked if I would attend as well. The following week we both attended the Living Waters service.

Since that time, we have grown stronger spiritually. We have established a more personal relationship with God. Over the next several months, we shared our story and journey with our pastor and his wife. They have been totally supportive and have provided us with a great deal of comfort and insightful perspective.

After all we had been through, and were continuing to experience, it would have been very easy to feel bitter resentment. Our pastor advised against giving permission to anyone to upset us. It has helped us both keep many things in perspective. At no time have we felt sorry for ourselves.

Forgiveness is important because we do not live in a perfect world.

Forgiveness turns negative emotions into positive ones. Forgiveness is a choice and, once we realize that we can forgive, our hearts can begin to heal.

Forgiveness includes the word "give." Grace and forgiveness are Christianity's greatest gift to the world. It is sad that so many do not partake of either.

I can tell you from personal experience that it is not easy to forgive. It may take some time, but forgiveness is the most precious of gifts, both to give and to receive. It is found deep within our hearts. Hopefully, more people will be willing to give it away.

CHAPTER 25

———

ON JULY 9, 2014, WE WERE INDICTED IN THE United States District Court in the Middle District of Florida, Fort Myers Division.

The indictment talked about Capitol Investments, some of the investor civil suits filed against me, the November 2009 Chapter 7 bankruptcy petition filed against Capitol by numerous investors, and the cash withdrawals we made in March and April of 2010. It also referred to the safe deposit box.

Count one of the indictment alleged a conspiracy between my wife and myself to evade a transaction reporting requirement.

Count two alleged "structuring" transactions to evade a reporting requirement.

Count three alleged concealment of property belonging to the estate of a bankruptcy debtor. It alleged that I fraudulently concealed from the Chapter 11 bankruptcy trustee the safe deposit box that my wife had established in 2010.

Count four alleged that my alleged failure to disclose the safe deposit box constituted a false declaration, certificate, verification, or statement in relation to bankruptcy proceedings. It alleged that I "knowingly and fraudulently" concealed the existence of my wife's safe deposit box.

The indictment included a forfeiture section. The allegations contained in counts one, three and four were incorporated by reference for the purpose of obtaining forfeitures pursuant to the United States Code.

For violations alleged in count two, it requested forfeiture of all of our money that we had withdrawn from our bank account in March and April 2010.

Further, for the alleged violations in counts three and four, it requested punishment by imprisonment for more than one year and forfeiture of all interest in any property, real or personal, which constitutes, or is derived from, proceeds traceable to the withdrawals.

CHAPTER 26

FROM 2009 THROUGH 2011, BOTH THE FBI AND the IRS, along with the US attorney's office in Newark, New Jersey, thoroughly investigated my involvement and role in Capitol Investments. Those investigations concluded that I was a victim of the Shapiro fraud, not a conspirator. The investigations further concluded that, because of Shapiro's schemes, I lost millions of dollars.

When I was first told that we were being criminally investigated for structuring, I had to research the term to determine what it meant. I asked one of my closest friends, a civil attorney who had been practicing law for 45 years, if he had ever heard of "structuring." He said he had no idea that such a crime existed. His initial reaction, when he read the description of the statute, was that it surely was a crime that arose upon the deposit of unexplained cash in an attempt to conceal an illegal source. He could not believe that it would apply to people moving their own legitimate funds from their bank account to a safe deposit box.

Obviously, he was wrong. The language of the statute does not distinguish between laundering drug money and withdrawing personal legitimate funds.

The withdrawals from Lorie's bank account, upon which the structuring charge was based, occurred in March and April of 2010. Shortly after, I was informed that I was being investigated by the IRS in connection with my tax returns. On November 4, 2010, all my banking records, including the records of the withdrawals in March and April 2010, were turned over to the IRS in New Jersey.

In the first few months of 2011, in connection with my bankruptcy proceeding under Chapter 11, I testified in detail about these withdrawals at my 341 hearings. The specific withdrawals were identified and discussed in the Chapter 11 trustee's written supplemental report filed with the court on July 11, 2011.

In September 2011, I pled guilty in Newark to one count of submitting an inaccurate tax return. Following a presentence investigation, and reports to the court, I was sentenced to one year and one day in federal prison.

The US attorney's office in Newark determined what charges should be filed against me with full knowledge concerning the March and April 2010 cash withdrawals. The sentencing judge had the ability to consider such uncharged conduct in determining the appropriate sentence on the tax conviction.

I served my sentence and was released. I served my period of supervised probation and was released. More than four years after all the information concerning the "structuring" offense had been fully disclosed to the US Attorney, FBI, and IRS, a US attorney in Florida filed "structuring" charges.

It seems unfair and unjust to consider the same "structuring" events in two separate sentencings. It seems unfair and unjust to use a four-year delay in instituting charges, and then to impose sentencing guidelines against me as a previously convicted felon. Nevertheless, this is what happened.

I have been told that a grand jury will indict a ham sandwich. Grand jury hearings are held in secret. A potential defendant is not informed of these proceedings. He cannot have an attorney present or present his side of the facts. The grand jury hears only the prosecutor's version of what happened. It is easy to see why so many people are indicted.

When the "structuring" allegation first surfaced, I met with my original criminal defense attorney in Naples. He showed me two pieces of paper. One sheet of paper listed the cash withdrawals in March and April of 2010. The other was a copy of the signatory cards for the safe deposit box. When Lorie and I met with our new attorneys in Naples, the government's discovery had now expanded to include 10 banker boxes of documents. There were more than 15,000 pages. We were stunned to see that much documentation. Illustrative of a bureaucracy with an unlimited budget, the government had gone back 25 years looking for information. Our attorney was holding an 8.5 x 11 folder in his hand. He said that, after reviewing all the documents, this folder contained the only relevant information.

CHAPTER 27

THE CIVIL LITIGATION WAS CONTINUING IN full swing. The plaintiff's attorneys were also working with an unlimited budget. I believe the plaintiff himself had little input into the actions taken by his attorneys. During his deposition, the plaintiff reaffirmed that he had not been aware that the lawsuit had been filed initially. He further stated that he was not aware of, nor had he read, the complaint prepared by his attorneys.

Throughout his deposition, he stated that he relied on his own financial advisors when making investments in Capitol. Through his advisers, he performed his own due diligence.

The plaintiff's Chief Financial Officer acknowledged in deposition that he was fooled by Shapiro. He believed Capitol to be a legitimate business.

Unbeknownst to me until his deposition, he wired Capitol another million dollars, after_Capitol had defaulted on the original investment.

The plaintiff owns multiple homes. He has his own private jet and hangar. He owns a Rolls- Royce, and Mercedes Benz. He calls $500,000 "half a stack" and $1 million "a full stack." I was told that he said he would probably give to charity anything he collected from his litigation against me.

The plaintiff appeared to take little interest in the details of the litigation. He never appeared at any of the multiple depositions. He assigned to his wife $10 of the $8.5 million dollars he was requesting, so she could attend all the depositions. For reasons, I still do not understand, she seemed to be primarily focused on inflicting pain and suffering and trying to destroy our marriage and our relationship with each other.

It appeared she had formed a social friendship with one of her attorneys. She told my attorney that they had lunch and went shopping together on multiple occasions. After lunch and shopping, they traveled to Fort Myers to attend my wife's criminal hearing. I can't think of any reason why she would travel to another city to attend this hearing except that she wanted to see Lorie's humiliation first hand, as Lorie was brought into the courtroom, handcuffed, shackled and manacled.

If this was the reason, I hope she got her $10 Worth.

CHAPTER 28

Remember that joy is not dependent on your circumstances. Some of the world's most miserable people are those whose circumstances seem most enviable. People who reach the top of the ladder career-wise are often surprised to find emptiness awaiting them. True joy is a byproduct of living in My Presence.

Therefore, you can experience it in palaces, in prisons.... Anywhere.

Do not judge a day as devoid of joy just because it contains difficulties. Instead, concentrate on staying in communication with Me. Many of the problems that clamor for your attention will resolve themselves. Other matters you must deal with, but I will help you with them. If you make problem-solving secondary to the goal of living close to Me, you can find joy even your most difficult days.

Habakkuk 3:17-19; 1 Chronicles 16:27

SINCE THE INDICTMENT IN JULY 2014, WE HAD been spending a great deal of time meeting with our attorneys. It was expensive, and we could ill afford it. Concurrently, we were dealing with the Ohio bankruptcy trustee regarding the sale of the house. We also had weekly, sometimes daily, motions filed against us in the civil litigation. It was an incredibly stressful time.

During this time, I was working with a real estate associate in Chicago, and tenant representative in Minnesota, to market and sell multiple real estate properties located in different states. These were properties that had been acquired in 2006. We were attempting to return capital to our investors. Needless to say, I was dealing with a lot of moving parts.

As we spent more time with our criminal defense attorneys, we became increasingly concerned about the risks of going to trial. The combination of an obscure criminal statute open to boundless interpretation and the lack of a "mens rea" requirement gave us great concern. Our attorneys said they would represent us to the best of their abilities but, at the end of the day, there were no guarantees. At the end of the day, whatever the outcome, they would be going home to their families.

My attorney was in Miami. Lorie's attorney was in Fort Myers. Lorie and I spent more time with her attorney because of proximity. Lorie's attorney had been a former prosecutor in Fort Myers and had a working relationship with all the attorneys involved. He mentioned on more than one occasion that "there was no place in the prison system for Lorie." He said that, if he asked the prosecutor for her best deal, she would probably agree to five years' probation for Lorie.

We were greatly concerned about the threatened criminal for-feiture payment. On more than one occasion, we made it very clear to Lorie's attorney that we were not able to make a forfeiture pay-ment. All the cash that was withdrawn in 2010 had been spent on bills and legal defenses. The only unencumbered asset we had left was Lorie's home. We told Lorie's lawyer that we would go to trial rather than accept a deal that would leave us homeless. He assured us, on multiple occasions, that he understood, and that there would be no agreed forfeiture.

With our limited resources depleted by the litigation, we were forced to confront the hard reality of our circumstances. Because I could no longer afford to defend the civil litigation, I entered into a voluntary judgment with the plaintiff in April 2015. The agreement stated that I denied ALL claims asserted by the plaintiff in the litigation. The agreement included the statement that my actions had been "willful and malicious." I was told that this statement was necessary only to prevent me from discharging the settlement by filing personal bankruptcy. I was assured by my attorney that this language would not be used for any other purpose. As I would soon find out, this was not true.

CHAPTER 29

IN RETROSPECT, I SHOULD NEVER HAVE ENTERED into a voluntary judgment. I did not have the funds to pay for an attorney at trial. I should have represented myself "pro se" as I did in Ohio. The plaintiff and his Chief Financial Officer had been deposed. They would have been my best witnesses. Hindsight is 20/20, but the stress of ongoing litigation was taking its toll.

Armed with this voluntary judgment, the plaintiff's attorneys pursued a course of collection proceedings unlike anything I, or any of my attorneys, had ever seen, anticipated, or experienced.

As we continued to have meetings with our attorneys regarding the criminal allegations, we were becoming increasingly aware of our untenable situation. Our previous criminal defense attorneys were correct when they stated, "it is not a level playing field."

Justice is not blind. It is lazy. Few defendants have millions to spend on legal defense. You are never going to outspend the government with its unlimited resources.

Judges are not happy when cases go to trial because a plea agreement was turned down. In many cases that go to trial, a defendant is given the maximum sentence, rather than the significantly lesser sentence that could have been obtained in a plea agreement.

We were, at most, in technical violation of a federal criminal statute. But the sentencing guidelines were based on the intent of the statute, not on how it was being applied to us. We were subject to a $250,000 dollar fine and five years' imprisonment for withdrawing our own funds from our own checking account to pay for our own legitimate expenses. Jurors are prohibited from knowing the sentencing guidelines.

Our attorneys had requested that we be allowed to self-surrender, but they were unable to get a commitment from the US Attorney's Office. We lived in continuous fear of US Marshals coming to our home, guns drawn, handcuffing us, and taking us to jail. We were also concerned for the safety of our small dog, should these events occur. Our attorney told us that, unfortunately, he had seen this happen too many times. After months of negotiation, we were allowed to self-surrender to US Marshals on February 26, 2015 at the Federal Courthouse in downtown Fort Myers.

We met with the US Marshals at the front steps of the courthouse. We were then escorted down to the basement of the building. First, they placed ankle shackles on my wife and then on me. We were fingerprinted, and a DNA sample was taken. We were told we could now spend some "me time," and they locked us into separate holding cells. A short time later, they came back to get us because they were having difficulty finding a code to enter for our criminal offense. They said this was a first. They had never heard of "structuring." We explained the offense, but I don't think they ever found an appropriate code. We were put back in our separate holding cells to wait for our court appearance.

Approximately 2 hours later, we were taken from our holding cells. We were placed in handcuffs that were shackled to a manacle around our waist. We were taken up in an elevator which opened into the courtroom. The only people in the courtroom, besides our attorneys, was the plaintiff's wife and attorney in the civil litigation. We were forced to remain handcuffed and shackled during the entire court hearing.

After the hearing, we were both released on an unsecured financial condition. We were instructed to report the first Wednesday of each month to the United States Pretrial Services Office located in the courthouse. We were required to surrender our passports. Our travel was restricted to the Middle and Southern District of Florida. We were told that home visits would be conducted throughout our period of supervision.

During the next several months, our attorneys continued negotiating with the US attorney's office, but were unable to reach an acceptable settlement.

CHAPTER 30

FACED WITH FRIGHTENING REALITIES AND LACK of finances to continue the litigation defense, we entered into a plea agreement in October of 2015.

We were forced to accept responsibility for something we never thought was illegal, in return for a downward departure recommendation from the sentencing guidelines. Welcome to the system.

Because of our acceptance of responsibility, a three-level reduction in the sentencing guidelines was recommended. An additional level of reduction was recommended for the timely submission of financial information.

If there was no adverse information, sentencing at the "low end" of the guidelines was recommended.

The plea agreement addressed forfeiture of assets. It included a money judgment in the amount of the funds we had withdrawn. This was the issue that had concerned us. I sent an email to Lorie's attorney asking for clarification and he advised us that it was just "boilerplate" language.

Because there were no victims, we were not required to pay restitution.

It was explained to us that the court was neither a party to, nor bound by, our plea agreement. The court could accept or reject the agreement or defer a decision until it had an opportunity to consider the presentence report prepared by the United States Probation Office.

The parties were permitted to make recommendations and present arguments to the court, but the sentence would be determined solely by the court, with the assistance of United States Probation Office.

We had to acknowledge that any discussions between us, our attorneys, or other agents for the government, regarding any recommendations by the government, were not binding on the court. We had to agree that, even if any of the recommendations were rejected, we would not be permitted to withdraw from the plea agreement. We had to expressly waive the right to appeal any sentence, even if the court erred in determining the applicable guideline range pursuant to the United States sentencing guidelines. We were waiving all our constitutional rights.

CHAPTER 31

OUR FOUNDING FATHERS UNDERSTOOD THAT tyranny wasn't likely to come from a foreign invasion. It would come from the step-by-step erosion of our freedoms by an expanding government. If the government wants to "get you," it can.

I don't believe anyone knows exactly how many federal laws exist that can trip up and imprison unwary citizens.

There are more than 300,000 criminal offenses listed in the 80,000-page Code of Federal Regulations.

It is a federal crime to walk a dog on federal lands with a leash longer than 6 feet. Violators can be fined and sentenced up to six months in prison.

An 11–year-old girl in Virginia, who saved a woodpecker from a cat, was fined for "transporting" a protected species.

A fisherman who threw back some undersized fish was convicted of violating the anti-shredding clause of the Sarbanes-Oxley Act. The Supreme Court overturned the conviction in a 5 to 4 vote.

An Alaskan fisherman sold 10 otters to a person he thought was an Alaskan native. The buyer was not an Alaskan native. Selling otters to non-Alaskan natives is a felony. The fisherman was forced to plead guilty to a felony.

George F. Will, a columnist for the Washington Post and Newsweek, wrote "there are an estimated 4500 federal criminal statutes and innumerable regulations backed by criminal penalties. Their sheer number would mean that Americans would not have a clear notice of what behavior is proscribed or prescribed. If you are being sent to prison for excavating arrowheads on federal land without a permit, your cellmate might have accidentally driven his snowmobile onto land protected by the Wilderness Act."

Bureaucrats and prosecutors love this criminalization binge.

Laws written in vague and ambiguous language give bureaucrats and prosecutors oppressive discretionary powers.

The government targets non-rich individuals, because they are more likely to cop a plea when faced with criminal charges. They certainly do not have the resources to defend themselves.

We have a criminal justice system with too many opportunities for generating defendants, too few restrictions on prosecutors, and ongoing corrosion of morality of law.

Until the government is required to prove criminal intent, or until congress decides to make changes, the prisons will keep filling up.

CHAPTER 32

———

LORIE'S SENTENCING DATE WAS JANUARY 25, 2016. During all our discussions, her criminal defense attorney stated that there was no place in the prison system for Lorie.

Many of our friends and family members had written letters of support.

Two letters outlined the chronology of the events leading up to the withdrawal of funds. Lorie's attorney said those two letters were "spot on." They told the story that needed to be told to the court. He assured us that he would tell it, and that the letters would be filed with the pre-sentence investigation report (PSI).

Unfortunately, he never submitted the letters to the court. The chronology of events, specifically all the disclosures made in 2011, were never communicated to the court.

The prosecutor noted only that the money was not found during the investigation. She confirmed that it was not moved to another bank account. She stated that "the money was gone." It was never communicated to the court that all the money had been previously disclosed. The court was not told that it was disclosed to all creditors during the 341 hearings and to the Justice Department and IRS when I completed my financial disclosure form in 2011. The court was not told that no one in the government, at that time, indicated or even alleged that it was a crime, nor did they try to confiscate the money.

The court was not told that the indictment did not come down until four years later, after the money had been spent on legal bills and living expenses. Had these facts been communicated to the court, there might have been a more favorable outcome. We will never know.

Lorie personally filed the letters written on her behalf with the court, after her sentencing, when she discovered that her lawyer had not filed them. She wanted them to be part of her record, but that ship had already sailed.

The government acknowledged that Lorie had no criminal history. The government's primary focus seemed to be securing a money judgment in the amount of $332,500.

The judge stated that the court was required to impose a sentence that is sufficient, but not greater than necessary, after considering all the factors. He stated that he had been sentencing people for a long time, and that "it's always difficult for someone such as yourself, who appears in federal court with no prior criminal history. I don't even remember a traffic offense or any minor criminal offense. I think, literally, you have no criminal history."

He stated "for six weeks, or five or six weeks in your life, it sounds like, on almost a daily basis, you engaged in conduct which resulted in the 332 some odd thousand dollars being taken out of your account and going somewhere. You did that in violation of federal law. You did that in the context that is mentioned in the presentence report as well as the conduct that your attorney has mentioned, and the government has mentioned."

The judge stated that he was obligated to impose a sentence upon Lorie, as an individual, for the offense committed and not for other reasons. He stated "I do think both specific details are relevant, although I tend to agree that I wouldn't really expect to see you back again. I think general deterrence also is important. I wouldn't have expected to see you here in the first place, given the profile of your background and your experience."

After considering all factors, the court agreed to grant, in part, Lorie's attorney's request for a variance, but not to the extent that he had requested. The government moved to dismiss count one of the indictment, which motion was granted.

The court stated, "It's the judgment of the court that you be committed to the custody of the Bureau of Prisons, to be imprisoned for a term of one year and one day." Upon completion of that sentence, Lorie was to be placed on supervised release for a term of two years. The mandatory drug testing requirements of the Violent Crime Control Act were waived, but she was required to submit to random drug testing, not to exceed 104 tests per year.

Other than the 100-dollar mandatory special assessment fee, there was no fine imposed, no victims identified, and no restitution required. It was all about a forfeiture money judgment.

CHAPTER 33

———

Adversity is the diamond dust Heaven polishes its jewels with.

— Thomas Carlyle

AT 10:45 AM, THE HEARING CONCLUDED. Needless to say, we were stunned.

Even the people we had reported to in pretrial services expressed their condolences and were shocked with the outcome. They thought Lorie would be sentenced to home detention or a period of probation. They were familiar with our story and surprised that it had not been told.

We thought the day couldn't get any worse. We were wrong. Plaintiffs' attorney in the civil suit, thought this would be a good time to file an ex-parte motion for issuance of a break order in aid of execution, which was granted by the court.

Ex parte is Latin for "one party." It refers to motions, hearings or orders at which only one party is heard. This is an exception to the basic rule that both parties must be present at any argument before a judge, and that an attorney may not communicate with a judge about a matter without previously notifying the opposition. Ex parte matters are usually temporary orders (like a restraining order or temporary custody order) pending a formal hearing.

Most jurisdictions require at least a diligent attempt to contact the other party's lawyer at the time and place of any ex parte hearing.

It seems to me this type of request would run contrary to the 5th and 14th amendments to the U.S. Constitution requiring that "no person shall be deprived of life, liberty, or property, without due process of law." A bedrock feature of due process should be fair notice to any party who may be affected by a legal proceeding. To me, this request and order would seem to violate the Constitution. Apparently not. This seems to be the new normal.

Ex parte judicial proceedings are usually reserved for urgent matters where requiring notice would subject one party to irreparable harm. A person suffering abuse at the hands of a spouse or significant other, for example, may seek an ex parte order from a court, directing the alleged abuser to stay away from him or her.

Our situation did not involve an urgent matter where requiring notice to us would subject plaintiff in the civil litigation to irreparable harm. The timing of this filing was just another mean-spirited, vitriolic attempt to disrupt our lives.

The ex parte motion was granted. It allowed the sheriff to use any force reasonably necessary to enter our home.

The sheriff was authorized to open and inspect all rooms, file cabinets, furniture, drawers, cabinets, closets, safes, or other enclosures or containers therein. He was authorized to seize all personal belongings and tangible property that I, as judgment debtor, owned.

The plaintiff's legal counsel and representatives were authorized to accompany the sheriff and to enter our property and to be present during the period required for the sheriff to seize and secure all my personal belongings and tangible property.

What if we were not home? We had a small 4-pound Maltese dog. What concern for his safety would be exercised if we were not there? The house was owned by my wife, not me. If we were not there, how could they determine what was my property and what was not. The break order did not provide for any safeguards. They would be left to do as they pleased.

Our attorney was not notified until after the motion was granted. The order was signed on January 22, 2016 without any hearing and without any notice to, or participation by, us.

What possible basis would plaintiff justify applying to the court for extraordinary relief without any notice to, or opportunity to be heard by, us in defense of the verified motion? We were left without any opportunity to object or check the facts presented to the court. The final judgment had been entered more than eight months earlier, after an amicable settlement of the case. Since that time, the plaintiff had taken exhaustive discovery in aid of execution, including issuance of writs of attachments to third party banks, depositions of myself and Lorie, and disclosure of all my financial information.

There are many examples of plaintiff's overzealous attempt to disrupt our lives. One stands out. I received a letter on November 25, 2015 from my personal bank. The account at this bank was my only personal checking account. It was used for the sole purpose of receiving my monthly social security checks. I was notified that a writ of garnishment had been placed on my account.

The letter further advised me that the bank and the bank's legal representatives were unable to give me any legal advice regarding this notice.

On December 11, 2015, I submitted a claim of exemption and request for hearing to my bank. Plaintiff's attorneys knew the funds (social security) were exempt from garnishment but had filed the writ anyway. The amount garnished was $2.06. It was subsequently returned to me as exempt funds. Plaintiff's attorneys spent thousands of dollars to pursue this exempt two dollars. This speaks volumes about the intent of this civil litigation.

There was similarly no legitimate purpose in applying for an ex parte break order permitting the sheriff to use force, if necessary, to break into our home.

CHAPTER 34

THE EX PARTE ORDER PERMITTED THE SHERIFF, among other things, to seize all computers, cell phones, iPads and other electronic devices and equipment.

Apparently, it did not matter that these devices contained confidential attorney client communications with our criminal defense attorneys and our civil attorneys relating to plaintiff's case and other pending legal matters.

The order allowed the sheriff to seize all my tangible property, including documents, instruments, and papers of value. I was working to sell various commercial properties to return capital to our investors. I needed all these documents to pursue this goal. The sheriff was authorized to simply seize everything, whether or not it had any financial value to the plaintiff.

We argued that the motion was improper because it did not limit the number of times the sheriff could "break" into, or otherwise gain access to, our home. It did not limit when these actions could be undertaken, day or night. We had a reasonable fear that the plaintiff would use the ex parte order simply to harass us.

We argued that the plaintiff was a very wealthy individual and that all his collection activities appeared designed to harass and to be vindictive, especially given the plaintiff's knowledge about our other legal troubles and financial status.

We argued that, with no limitation in scope or duration, the order was an improper invasion of our right to privacy and operated as an improper taking of Lories property.

The order allowed the sheriff to seize all the personal property the plaintiff listed on the order's attached exhibit. A substantial majority of the listed property was owned by Lorie.

Contemporaneously with filing for Chapter 11 bankruptcy, we were advised to identify, and have appraised, all our jointly held personal property. The ownership of martial property is commonly referred to as "tenants by the entirety." "Entireties" property is property owned by husband and wife. Each spouse has an undivided interest. In essence, each owns the entire estate.

Holding title to property as "tenants by the entirety" gives the spouse protection from creditors. Husband and wife are treated as a single legal entity. Creditors cannot seize such assets for debts in just one spouse's name. Under Florida law, jointly owned property is not subject to attachment or seizure as a means of collecting a debt against one spouse.

The break order allowed the sheriff to seize all the listed items, including steak knives, rugs, furniture, dog beds, the dog closet, clothes and a small lamp.

The order expressly authorized plaintiffs' counsel to accompany the sheriff to seize property. My attorney was not afforded the opportunity to attend the sheriff's seizure.

We were given no opportunity to be heard in opposition to the order. There was not even a telephonic conference held to discuss the issues.

On Thursday, January 28, 2016, two sheriff's deputies and plaintiff's attorneys came to our home. Fortunately, we were there. The sheriff showed me the break order that allowed them to enter our home. I called my attorney, who was in Fort Lauderdale, and told him what was going on. He said he wanted to talk to plaintiff's attorney and asked me to hand him the phone. When I handed the phone to plaintiff's attorney, he hung up on my attorney and said he "didn't have time to talk."

One of plaintiff's attorneys was going through the entire house opening all drawers, cabinets, and closets. He was videotaping everything on his iPad. The other attorney was clearly enjoying this total invasion of our privacy. He was verbally abusive to my wife and said that, after this visit, he would be back with a bigger truck and take everything, and that she could think about that when she was sitting in prison.

They took our furniture. They took family pictures, my grandfather's hand-written poems, all my personal paperwork, a car seat for my dog and all my clothes.

Plaintiff's attorney thought it was funny to leave me one golf shirt hanging in the closet. He took a souvenir photo of it hanging in the closet. Because I had to be in court in three days for my sentencing, my wife requested that I be allowed to keep at least one outfit to wear to court: a shirt, pants, shoes and sport coat. Plaintiff's attorney said "no," and told the movers to "take it all."

CHAPTER 35

PLAINTIFF'S ATTORNEYS IN THE CIVIL LITIGA-
tion filed an objection to set aside my plea agreement. My criminal
defense attorney's response was "what the F---?" He had never heard
of an objection to a plea agreement from a plaintiff in a civil lawsuit.
The plaintiff alleged he was a victim and wanted to have input into
my sentencing.

During my sentencing on Monday, February 1, 2016, one of the
plaintiff's attorneys interrupted the court. She had filed a "victim"
statement on behalf of the plaintiff and wanted to be heard before the
court issued the sentence.

The court asked the government if the plaintiff was a "victim" within the meaning of the victim impact statute. The government stated it did not believe the plaintiff was a victim in this case.
The prosecutor confirmed that this plaintiff had not even filed his
civil lawsuit until 2012, and the civil judgment was not obtained
until 2015.

While plaintiff's attorneys tried to prejudice the court by associating me with the Capitol Ponzi scheme, the prosecutor confirmed
that I was not charged in that scheme.

Plaintiff's attorney finally conceded that her client was not a
"victim" of the structuring violation for which I pled guilty, but she

still asked the court to consider a harsher sentence. She requested the court exceed the guidelines to order a firmer sentence.

Plaintiffs' attorney stated that the voluntary judgment in favor of her client acknowledged that I "willfully and maliciously" persuaded her client to invest. That was the pledge that I had been assured was only to prevent the judgment from being discharged in bankruptcy. Now it was leveraged to try to get a longer criminal sentence for me.

I was sentenced to one year and a day in federal prison, followed by supervised release for a term of three years. The mandatory drug testing requirements of the Violent Crime Control Act were waived. The government's motion to dismiss counts two, three, and four of the indictment was granted, and those counts were dismissed.

The government asked for a forfeiture money judgment in the amount of $332,500 that would be a joint and severable liability. In the final analysis, it was all about the money.

This was not a liability we had anticipated. The funds were not confiscated when they were originally disclosed and available in 2011. The money had been spent, and a lien was now being placed on our only remaining asset: our home.

CHAPTER 36

———

BECAUSE THE CIVIL COURT HAD FAILED TO LIMIT the scope of the plaintiff's ex parte order, plaintiff's attorneys came back. They hired two shifts of off-duty police officers to sit in my neighbor's driveway all night long to watch the house on Monday, February 22, 2016. I noticed them sitting there while I was walking our dog. I asked the officer if everything was okay. I asked if something had happened in the neighborhood that I should be concerned about. He said, "No. Nothing to worry about."

The next morning, at approximately 9 AM, plaintiff's attorneys showed up again at the house, accompanied by two sheriff's deputies and a large moving truck with a crew of several movers. Once again, we were fortunate that we were home, if only for the safety of our small dog. The sheriff showed me the break order which authorized them to enter our home. Once again, I called our attorney and advised him they were back. Once again, plaintiff's attorneys refused to talk to my attorney. It was now obvious that the sheriff's deputies sitting in our neighbor's driveway all night was just to further harass and embarrass us.

My wife was required to self-surrender to the Coleman Federal Prison on February 26, 2016. I was required to report on March 4, 2016 to the federal prison facility in Pensacola Florida. The timing of this latest raid on our home was to ensure that all our remaining furniture would be taken before we had to report. Plaintiff's attorney was making good on his previous threat that we would know that we would have nothing to come home to when our sentences were completed. Except for my wife's clothes, they took everything.

We had requested, that any property that belonged to my wife, including personal property that was owned by the "entireties", be identified and inventoried before being seized. That would allow opportunity for the issue to be adjudicated. Our request was ignored.

CHAPTER 37

———

There are unimaginable depths that are released or developed in those who have had to face and cope with diversities and pressures.

Otherwise, one might remain shallow and superficial and have no clue of what they are really capable of becoming.

— Author unknown

THIS WAS NOW THE SECOND TIME IN JUST A FEW weeks that the plaintiffs' attorneys and deputy sheriffs had come to our home. Try to imagine living in an atmosphere where there is no limit to the number of times someone can break into, or otherwise gain access to, your home. These actions could be undertaken, unannounced, anytime, day or night.

It was clear that they were here this time to take everything. The sheriff explained to me that the break order, (as explained to him by the plaintiff's attorney), allowed them to take anything they wanted except for my wife's clothes. The plaintiff's attorneys were instructing the movers, on a room by room basis, to take everything. They threw my wife's clothes on the floor as they emptied all the dressers. Her feminine and personal hygiene products were thrown into the sink as they went through each bathroom. This was very difficult to watch. I told my wife she should probably leave for the day and that I would stay home and take care of our dog. She left with the understanding that I would call her when they were finished.

The movers were apologetic and polite. One told me this was not the first time they had to do this. When they were going through the kitchen, taking all our pots, pans, glasses and silverware, they started to take a container that held our dog's food. I asked the mover to please leave it for the obvious reason. He said he would ask plaintiff's attorney if it was okay to leave it. He came back and apologized but said he was told to take everything.

As this process continued throughout the morning, I noticed one of the plaintiff's attorneys in my wife's closet. She was going through my wife's purse. I asked her to please leave my wife's personal items alone. She ignored my request.

She put the safe deposit box key she took from my wife's purse into her pocket. I asked her to please put it back, but she ignored my request. Because we were leaving in a few days to report to federal prison, we needed access to the safe deposit box to secure papers and personal effects before we left. We now had to hire a locksmith to break into our safe deposit box.

When plaintiff's other attorney was in the master bath, I ask him to please leave my prescription medications. I had just purchased a three-month supply and one had been expensive. That request also was denied.

At this point, plaintiff's attorneys became tired of me asking for certain considerations. They told the sheriff to tell me that I had to wait outside while they continued telling the movers what to take. I told the sheriff that I felt I had a right to remain in the house and see what was being taken. He said, "I'm only going to tell you one time: Take your dog and wait outside." "This court order," he said, "allows them to take anything they want." I was then forced to wait outside, while plaintiffs' attorneys ransacked our home.

It is difficult writing this. I hate reliving that day. It was unimaginably difficult to watch 20 years of belongings being packed up and moved out of our home. Plaintiff's attorneys seemed to be enjoying it. They ordered lunch to be brought to the house.

After lunch, one of plaintiff's attorneys started walking around the outside of the house. He noticed that we had some pottery sitting in the landscape. He picked it up and loaded it on the truck. He also pulled out of the ground the solar landscape lighting that was in front of the house. He told the movers to disconnect and take the washer and dryer, as they were finishing up for the day. Everything was taken.

After approximately 8 hours, a second truck and a new crew came in to relieve the morning workers. The moving process took approximately 12 hours.

CHAPTER 38

————

ONCE THEY LEFT, I CALLED MY WIFE AND TOLD her to come home. When she walked in, she was stunned to see what all had been taken. She asked how they could take the washer and dryer that she purchased with the house. I had no answer.

It was now almost 9 o'clock at night. We needed to get to the grocery before they closed to buy dog food. They took our dog's food, car seat, and his beds. We needed a place to sleep. This was peak season and it was difficult to find a hotel, especially one that was dog friendly.

The only hotel we could afford was not dog friendly. Lorie had to report to prison in three days. I had to report the following week. We were forced to give our dog to a close friend to keep while we were gone.

"The heart misses most what it loved best."

This was a very painful decision. We hoped to remain a family for the short time we had left, but circumstances left us with no alternative.

CHAPTER 39

———

ON FRIDAY, FEBRUARY 26, 2016, WE LEFT EARLY IN the morning so that Lorie could report to the Coleman correctional facility. We had a close friend who came into town a day earlier to drive us to the facility. We all knew I would be in no shape to drive home.

We had gone through this separation process on February 14, 2012 when I reported to the Edgefield South Carolina facility. We never anticipated that we would have to go through this emotional roller coaster again. We had time to prepare ourselves for this eventuality. We both agreed that our faith would get us through the next few months. We would remain strong, and soon be a family again.

There were other people reporting at the same time. One of the security staff members came out to escort everyone into the facility. She was polite and courteous and gave me some comfort that everything would be okay.

We gave each other a final hug and kiss. With no tears, Lorie said she would be fine and that, hopefully, when I got to Pensacola, we would at least be able to email each other. In the meantime, we would both be talking with her mother. She was then told it was time to enter the facility, and we said our final goodbye.

I stayed emotionally strong all the way to the end of the sidewalk. It was unimaginable that we were going through this again.

Only this time, she was the one entering federal prison. It was a long three hours for my poor friend who had to drive me home.

When we got home, I went straight to the Christian bookstore and bought cards for our anniversary and birthdays that would occur while we were separated. Knowing I couldn't send her anything from prison, I wanted to write the cards in advance and give them to a friend to mail in April and July.

I had to report to Pensacola the following Friday, March 4, 2016.

Lorie and I were able to talk on the phone before I had to report. She told me that everyone she had met so far had been nice, considerate, and understanding. Her roommate was a CPA. I said, "That's good. It's not like we don't have some accounting issues." We were trying to maintain a sense of humor.

The number and length of phone calls was limited, but we spoke every day until I had to report. We were hopeful that we would be able to email each other soon. We agreed to stay in touch through Lorie's mother, in the meantime, Lorie assured me everything would be fine and that she hoped everything would work out well once I got to Pensacola.

Thursday, March 3, 2016, would be our last direct conversation until I was released to the halfway house on September 20, 2016.

CHAPTER 40

THURSDAY, MARCH 3, I FLEW TO PENSACOLA. I met the same friend who had driven us to Coleman. He had driven down from Atlanta. We had dinner and, the next morning, he drove me to the Federal Correctional Institute.

The Pensacola facility looked more like the satellite camp that I had expected. Unlike the facility at Edgefield, we could drive to the building to which I was to report. The Pensacola facility is a former Naval base. We had to go through a security checkpoint to enter the base, but security was less significant than at Edgefield.

Each inmate was assigned a counselor and case manager. My case manager and counselor were supportive and considerate. During my initial meeting, they asked me to explain why I was there. They were not familiar with the charge of "structuring." After I explained the charge, and that my wife was in Coleman for the same offense, my counselor's only comment was, "That's crazy." I said, "It may be crazy, but that's why I'm here." My case manager said she would do everything she could to get me released as soon as possible. "In the meantime," she said, "just make the best of your stay."

I was assigned to a third-floor housing unit. This was not an open dormitory. There were six bunkbeds located in a relatively small room. Twelve of us lived in a room designed for 4 to 6 people. I could literally touch the person sleeping on either side of me. During the mandatory standing counts, there was barely enough room for all of us to stand. With the door closed most of the time, the wall unit air conditioner kept the temperature very cold. My hands would become numb just trying to hold a book to read.

We were required to wear steel-toed boots from 8 AM to 4 PM. Walking up and down three flights of stairs, especially in those boots, was very difficult because I have arthritis in both knees. Between laundry, commissary, and having to report to various appointments, I was required to climb the steps dozens of times per day. I realized that I would not be physically able to maintain this routine. After a couple of weeks, I requested reassignment to a single-story building.

My case manager advised me that the only way I could be reassigned was through a medical waiver. When I asked the medical director for a waiver to be relocated, he said I had to get approval from my counselor. After a couple of weeks of this runaround, I finally found a sympathetic medical practitioner. She told me that the x-ray technician came in once a week and that she would order X- rays of my knees to confirm that I had arthritis. Surprisingly, I was called to medical a couple of hours later when the x-ray technician, unexpectedly, came into work. The x-rays were taken, and the arthritis was confirmed. This might be the quickest response to a medical request in BOP history. I was not going to look a gift horse in the mouth.

The BOP historically does not move very quickly. You can imagine my surprise when, that same week, I was given a "callout" to report to dental to get my teeth cleaned. I thought, "WOW! The process has certainly improved." I had not even requested a teeth cleaning. When I told the dental assistant and dentist that I was surprised to be getting my teeth cleaned, they said my record reflected that I had made this request. I told them I had not. They looked at the records and said I put in the request in February of 2012. That was when I had reported to Edgefield, 4 years earlier.

The PA issued me a medical waiver that provided for no prolonged standing or heavy lifting and asked that I be reassigned to a single-story building and given a lower bunk. I gave the waiver to my case manager who called the counselor in "A" building, which was the only single-story building available. He said because of the medical restriction, he had no choice but to move me immediately. Another inmate helped carry my personal effects to the new unit. Fortunately, there was one lower bunk available. The previous occupant had been sent to the county jail for an altercation with another inmate.

Unlike my previous housing unit, building "A" was an open dorm. The good news was that I no longer had to climb three flights of stairs or feel like I was living in a closet. The bad news was that there were now 14, rather than 12, inmates in the cubicle. There were seven bunkbeds and lockers in a 15 x 20 space.

It is a requirement that everyone assigned to the Bureau of Prisons be given a job assignment. Pensacola housed an average of 800 to 850 inmates. Most inmates were assigned jobs that required them to be transported each day to Eglin Air Force Base. The bus ride was an hour and a half each way. After a few weeks of medical orientation, I was assigned the job of CCI orderly. I had no idea what that was. I learned early that the only way to get information is from another inmate.

Access to my counselor and case manager was limited. Another inmate told me he was a CCI orderly. I asked what we were required to do. He said he had been a CCI orderly for three years and, so far, they had not asked him to do anything. I soon realized that this job was assigned to older inmates or inmates with medical restrictions. I qualified in both categories.

The Coleman facility, where Lorie was staying, was also a satellite camp.

There were two two-story buildings, divided into four units. Each unit housed approximately 100 inmates. There were no razor wire fences. During Lorie's stay, the facility averaged between 300 and 400 residents at any given time. Each floor was an open dormitory with individual cubicles. There was one bunk bed per cubicle. Lorie was assigned the upper bunk.

Through conversations with her mother, I learned that Lorie had been assigned a unit orderly job. Her job consisted of cleaning a recreation room that contained a computer area and some card tables. It took her about an hour a day, sometimes less, to clean her area. The balance of her day was spent taking classes and exercising. She participated in a book club and taught an ab exercise class. She took nutrition and Spanish classes.

Soon after Lorie arrived at Coleman, one of the TVs was not working properly. There was a line that cut off about 4 inches of the top of the screen. One of the girls said it always did that. Lorie said that she was good with electronics and asked to see the remote. After a few adjustments, Lorie corrected the problem. She later overheard one of the inmates saying, "That new girl? She can fix things."

It took approximately 3 months for us to get approval to email each other. The BOP moves at a glacial pace. Once we could email, Lorie confirmed that her release date was October 12, 2016. She would be reporting to a halfway house in Fort Myers. It was the same Salvation Army house to which I had been released in 2012.

In retrospect, our time in the BOP passed fairly quickly. We learned to get into a daily routine to occupy our time. Tasks that most people take for granted, became something to look forward to each day: Picking up laundry, going to the commissary, taking classes, spending time in the library, and exercising. Lorie walked six to nine miles each day. Sometimes more.

I had a similar routine. Because my job did not require me to do anything, I spent a great deal of time in the library reading and writing letters. I walked 4 to 6 miles most days. Fortunately, horizontal walking was not hard on my knees.

Vertical stairclimbing was the problem.

There was a daily laundry service. I could drop off my laundry early in the morning and pick it up the same day. Commissary visits were once a week.

Commissary lines were often long. I learned that I could move to the head of the line by giving my commissary list to the inmate who worked in the commissary the night before and letting him add something for himself.

CHAPTER 41

———

LORIE AND I BOTH SETTLED INTO ROUTINES. WE were learning how the system worked in our respective environments. We thought that being incarcerated would provide us with a break, or at least a buffer, from our other legal issues. Once again, we were wrong.

Prior to reporting to our respective facilities, we were fortunate enough to have a friend put money into each of our commissary accounts. Because we were limited in how much we could spend per month, we had what we thought was enough money to last us for the time we anticipated being there. Within a few weeks after Lorie arrived, the government froze Lorie's commissary account. A Motion for a Forfeiture to enforce Money Judgment had been filed.

We had been told that a Motion for a Forfeiture Money Judgment would be pursued only in cases where the funds had been acquired illegally or where the funds were used to acquire something illegal. Because neither was the case in our situation, we were assured we had nothing to worry about. The funds came from the federal government and were spent on legitimate living expenses and legal fees. There was never an allegation to the contrary. Once again, we had been misinformed.

Lorie's attorney, tried to get her commissary lien removed. It took several months to resolve.

Just when Lorie was about to leave Coleman, the frozen commissary funds became available.

The fact that Lorie and I were both incarcerated did not slow down the plaintiff's attorneys in the civil lawsuit. They continued to file motion after motion after motion. Just before we had to report to prison, plaintiff's attorneys filed an emergency motion to direct that I appear for a special examination. They continued to file motions trying to add Lorie to the suit, although she had never been a party.

Plaintiff's attorneys wanted to take our depositions while we were in prison.

They continued to file post judgment requests for production of documents, even though they had already seized all our records. Nice people.

After the break order, I filed, pursuant to Florida statute section 222.061 and 222.25, an affidavit to claim the four-thousand-dollar personal property exemption to which everyone's entitled. I identified $1400.00 of property that I wanted returned.

The court allowed the sheriff to segregate out, and not allow the sale of, the items I had identified. The judge said she would reserve ruling on whether I got those items back. In the interim, she was going to allow the special magistrate to review the papers and electronic devices for any attorney- client material.

We were hoping to finally have the opportunity to litigate whether property belonging to Lorie had been taken unjustly.

My attorney filed an emergency motion to stop the sale of the seized property and allow us time to adjudicate the issue. The judge would not postpone the sale unless I posted a bond for double the amount of the property's value. I had to post a bond in the amount of $40,000 just to be allowed a hearing. Once a bond was posted, the court agreed to conduct an evidentiary hearing on whether the property truly belonged to Lorie.

We strongly believed that we would win the argument. Under Florida law, all marital property is entireties property. I was able to have a business associate post a $40,000 cash bond several days prior to the sale date. We told the judge that it was important to us that any photos or family memorabilia, that had no monetary value to any-one else, be returned to us, or at least segregated from the sale at this point. We asked that my prescription medications be returned. The judge agreed to fashion relief that protected those items, if a bond was posted.

Plaintiff's attorney argued that Lorie should be required to produce documents. My attorney reminded the judge that it would be impossible for Lorie to produce any documents while she was in prison, and that all the documents requested had already been seized and were no longer in her custody, possession or control.

Plaintiff's attorney subpoenaed all my prior civil and crimi-nal attorneys (12 in total) to produce retainer agreements, billing records and source of payment documents.

CHAPTER 42

———

"Corn cannot expect justice from a court composed of chickens."

—African Proverb

THERE IS SUCH A FEELING OF HELPLESSNESS when incarcerated. I had no control over the events occurring in my life. I had limited access to email. I had limited phone minutes to even call my attorney. I had to schedule an attorney call several days, and sometimes weeks, in advance. There was one phone provided for attorney-client calls for almost 900 inmates.

I knew our emergency motion had been granted, and the bond had been posted. I was relieved that we would now at least be able to litigate that we owned our own property. It sounds ridiculous to even say that. It is hard to imagine a court ruling that no joint assets had been acquired in almost 20 years of marriage. My grandfather's handwritten poems, a painting that had been in my wife's family since she was born in Columbia, our wedding pictures, a poem written to me by a dear friend who passed away in 2003 and other items of no value, other than to us, could hopefully now be preserved.

That feeling of relief was short lived. Unbelievably, after granting our emergency motion giving us time to post a bond. The court allowed ALL our property to be sold a few days later. I was told the plaintiff purchased all the property for $10,000.

Why the court would allow everything to be sold has never been explained to me. My attorney was stunned.

The plaintiff's attorneys promptly filed a writ of garnishment against my associate who posted the bond. It cost him $4,000 in legal fees to get his own money back.

You can imagine my stress level in getting the required bond posted while being incarcerated, and the subsequent feelings of despair when ALL our property was sold.

My wife was informed that her safe deposit box had been forcibly opened on July 8, 2016. The contents had been removed and inventoried and were being stored in a vault at the branch location. We later learned that those contents had been relocated to another branch in the northern part of the state. We asked our attorney how this was possible. He said he was told the contents would be stored for several years specified by state law. If the contents were not retrieved within the statutory time period, the contents could be sold or disposed of according to state law. When asked again why it was opened in the first place, my attorney said the bank made some reference to the "Patriot Act," but nothing more specific.

Once Lorie was released to the halfway house in October, she contacted the bank and was able to retrieve all the contents that had been inventoried. No explanation was given as to why the contents were taken in the first place. We assume that it was at the direction of the US Attorney's Office, pursuing the forfeiture money judgment.

In the few months since we had reported to prison, we had lost all our furniture and household items, the contents of Lorie's safe deposit box had been confiscated, and Lorie's commissary account had been frozen. There was never any attempt to freeze my commissary account. No one says the system operates efficiently or logically.

We now had approximately two and three months respectively before we were to report to the halfway house in Fort Myers. The balance of our time was spent reading, exercising and pursuing our daily routines. We were thankful we could now email each other and stay in touch every few days. We looked forward to being together soon.

CHAPTER 43

_____

ON THE MORNING OF SEPTEMBER 20, 2016, I WAS released from the Pensacola facility and driven to the local airport. My friend who had originally dropped me off had purchased an airline ticket for me to get back to Fort Myers. Another friend picked me up at the Fort Myers airport and drove me to the halfway house. I was required to be there by 9 PM.

Most of the staff had changed since I had been there in 2012, but there were a couple of familiar faces. Once again, a photo ID was taken, I was given a breathalyzer and urinalysis test. I was given some sheets and a blanket and assigned to a room. It was the same room I had been assigned in 2012. Four people in the room shared one sink. There was an adjoining bath and shower which we shared with four other people.

I was assigned a case manager. He had been a case manager in the system for 17 years. Like my previous counselors, he was not familiar with "structuring." I told him my counselors at Pensacola told me I should be released to home confinement after a short orientation period of a week to 10 days. He told me I had been misinformed. I would not be eligible for home confinement until December 12, 2016, Lorie would not be eligible until December 16, 2016. I was not happy with the prospect of having to spend the next three months living at the Salvation Army. Our release dates from the BOP were January 9 and 13, respectively.

On the morning of October 12, 2016, Lorie was released from Coleman. One of our close friends drove to Coleman to pick her up and bring her to the halfway house. When she arrived later that afternoon, it was the first time we had seen each other in 30 weeks. Our reunion was very emotional. We were so happy to be together again, even under these circumstances,

CHAPTER 44

———

LORIE WAS FAMILIAR WITH THE HALFWAY HOUSE because of my brief stay there in 2012. She went through the same check-in procedure and was assigned a room two doors down from mine. The female federal inmates were assigned rooms at the end of the hallway. The state inmates were assigned to another wing of the building.

Everyone shared a common cafeteria. The federal and state inmates were separated as much as possible. Federal inmates were identified by different colored name badges. Federal and state inmates were not allowed to talk with each other, or sit with each other, in the cafeteria during dining hours. The federal men and women shared a common TV and lounge area.

After 5 PM, we could order carryout food from several of the local vendors.

There was a small outside laundry room that had not changed since 2012. It consisted of three washers and 3 dryers. Usually, two of them worked.

There was also a small outside common area where inmates could smoke.

This area was shared by federal and state residents at different assigned times.

Once we arrived in Fort Myers, we became a part of the Residential Reentry Program. The program is designed to help inmates who have been in prison for a long time relocate and adjust back into society. The program does not have a purpose for those incarcerated for a short time. Reentry, for us, should have consisted of recharging our cell phones.

The mandatory residential reentry classes that I was required to take in 2012 were apparently no longer required. The main focus seemed to be getting everyone a job. Once employed, we were required to pay 25% of our gross income to cover food and housing costs. Because of my age and some health restrictions, I was not required to seek employment. Lorie had not worked outside the home since 1997 and was not required to work either. When our counselor went to our home to approve the home setting, he saw that ALL of the furniture had been taken. We told him a friend was willing to purchase and loan us furniture until we could get back on our feet. Over the next several weeks, we were given periodic passes to accomplish this goal. We were allowed to keep our car at the facility so that Lorie could take me to various medical appointments. Our counselor had been in the business for many years and was sympathetic to our circumstance.

The notary who caused me problems in 2012 was still there. Once again, she would not accept my BOP photo ID to notarize my signature on a legal document sent from my attorney. Once again, I asked her if she thought I had someone else serving my time for me. Once again, I had to get a current driver's license before she would notarize my signature. Welcome back to the system.

My first month at the Salvation Army, I had to spend seven days a week at the facility. We were allowed approximately 45 minutes to an hour of exercise, most days. There was a small lot across the street where we could walk from 5 to 6 PM. The rest of my time was spent reading and watching TV.

After Lorie arrived, we were allowed to be on home confinement during the weekends. We could leave on Fridays around 4 o'clock and had to report back by 9 PM Sunday evening. Keeping us at the Salvation Army during the week was an unbelievable waste of the government's time and money. Most of the facility residents had been in prison for periods ranging from 10 to 20 years and needed a reentry adjustment period. We did not.

CHAPTER 45

———

ON DECEMBER 12 AND 16TH WE WERE ELIGIBLE
for home confinement.

Even though we had been released to the halfway house in
September and October of 2016, we were still under the umbrella
of the BOP until our final release dates in January of 2017. While we
were under the umbrella of the BOP, we were not allowed to receive
any benefits, including social security. We were not allowed to purchase health insurance. We were not allowed to have a credit card or
incur any debt. While medical services were available while we were
residents at Pensacola and Coleman, they were not available to us as
residents in the halfway house. We were allowed to make medical
appointments with doctors and dentists, but the BOP would not pay
any of the costs.

The government cancelled all my Social Security benefits once
I was incarcerated. It is a federal offense to receive Social Security
payments while under the umbrella of the BOP. Once I was released
and eligible to receive payments, I was charged a penalty for the can-
cellation. My counselor said, "I know this doesn't seem right, but
that's just the way it is."

As you can imagine, we were extremely happy to be leaving the
Salvation Army and headed back to our home. While we were on
home confinement, we were required to wear a GPS ankle bracelet

24 hour per day. It was attached to our ankles before leaving the facility. We could not take it off. It had to be worn at all times, even during a shower or bath. Anytime we had to go to the grocery, doctor appointment, dental appointment or anywhere else, we had to fill out a movement request form and obtain approval in advance. We called the facility when we left our home and when we arrived at our destination. We called when we left our destination and when we arrived back home.

We were not allowed to have any alcohol in our home. We were periodically called, generally in the evenings, and given one hour to report back to the facility for a breathalyzer test. It did not matter that we had been excused from any mandatory drug or alcohol testing. The system has a host of cottage industries that must be supported and maintained. Drug and alcohol testing, and GPS monitoring, are just examples. The BOP now employs more people than the FBI.

Even though we were wearing GPS monitoring devices, someone called each night between one and 3 o'clock in the morning to make sure we were there. What is the purpose of having to wear an ankle monitor if they are going to call me in the middle of the night?

We only had to endure this process for the 3 to 4 weeks we were on home confinement. Once our home confinement period concluded, we had three days to contact our probation officer. Our probation officer was the same person I had in 2012. She had met with us while we were at the halfway house and was familiar with our situation. Lorie had been given a two-year probationary period. I was given three.

Once contacted, our probation officer came to our home and explained what was required of us during our probationary periods. She explained the reporting form that we were required to complete each month online.

She confirmed that any requests to leave the middle district of Florida had to be approved by her in advance. Lorie asked if she could visit her mother in the Midwest. Our probation officer confirmed that no reasonable request would be denied. As of this writing, we are still on probationary status. Our probation officer has been understanding. No request has been denied.

CHAPTER 46

———

A diamond...

It once was nothing special,

But with enough pressure and time, Becomes spectacular.

— Solange Nicole

WHEN I REFLECT ON OUR INCREDIBLE JOURNEY, challenging as it has been, I am proud that we continued to survive each adversity. It would have been easy to give up, considering everything that was thrown at us. It has not been easy. There have been many moments of despair. But through each test and trial, we remained committed to our spiritual beliefs and each other. While many outside influences have tried to destroy our lives, we have become stronger and continue to experience new joy.

Our journey through the legal system confirms today's lack of personal responsibility, integrity and honesty. Look at what is going on every day in our government. The political and religious turmoil is unbelievable.

Whether or not you want to call it fake news, all of this continues to be fueled by the media. If Thomas Edison invented the light bulb today, the evening news headline would be "Tragedy strikes the candle industry."

We should have a good news channel (GNC). One that reports only on positive things that happen in the world. I have to believe there is more good than bad.

Paul Harvey Aurandt, better known as Paul Harvey, was an American radio broadcaster for ABC radio networks. He died in February of 2009, at the age of 90. One of his more memorable quotes was "if 'pro' is the opposite of 'con' what is the opposite of 'progress?'"

On a radio broadcast in 1965, he made startling predictions in a commentary titled "If I were the devil." The predictions he made 52 years ago, before social media, iPhones and many of the technologies we take for granted today, have all come true. I encourage everyone to Google, and listen to, his commentary.

Prisons do not rehabilitate. I met many people who had been sent back to prison because they had been provided with no skills and had no prospect of success. They were considered just other valueless life in the system.

Don't get me wrong. Many, if not most, are in prison because that is where they belong. Many are "bad" people determined to prey on others. They are locked away because of what they have done. Unfortunately, it is often difficult to separate the "bad" from those who deserve a second chance to do the right thing.

Fairness should be fundamental but, sadly, right and wrong have little to do with the law. The law gives prosecutors all the breaks. They can convict almost anyone for anything. Of all federal indictments, approximately 97% plead out. Do you think that's because 97% are guilty? Of course not. It is almost impossible for a defendant to win.

Sentencing guideline reform is much-needed. The guidelines should reflect the seriousness of the crime. Statutes should be more clearly written to reflect their intent, not open to unintended interpretations.

While changes are necessary, nothing will change. "The Business of American Injustice" is designed to perpetuate itself. These necessary reforms would not benefit its self-serving interests. Our criminal code has grown too large to manage and become too complicated to reform.

We have a two-tiered legal system. Those in the first group are often poor, with little resources to defend themselves. They are more likely to enter a plea agreement when faced with criminal charges.

Then there is the wealthy and politically connected group. Hillary Clinton is in a category all her own. While it is no way to run a criminal justice system, she's apparently too big to jail.

What would happen to me if I received a congressional subpoena to provide documents and information, then destroyed all the requested evidence, acid washed my computer, and took a hammer to 13 of my blackberry phones? I don't think that I would see the light of day for quite some time. They wanted to read her emails, not her book.

FBI Director Comey said Clinton was guilty of excessive carelessness which, by legal definition, translates to gross negligence. Gross negligence is an indictable offense, especially when dealing with sensitive classified materials. The statute does not require intent. Based upon Comey's findings, Clinton could not get a low-level security job at the state department, but she could still run for president.

We have since learned that Comey decided not to recommend an indictment prior to even having interviewed Clinton. Comey later confirmed that he was instructed by then Attorney General Loretta Lynch, to refer to the Clinton investigation as a "matter" rather than "investigation." We will probably never know what former President Clinton and Attorney General Lynch discussed in her plane for just under an hour, on the tarmac, while Hillary was being investigated. Maybe Lynch was asking how to turn one thousand dollars into one hundred thousand dollars in 10 months by trading cattle futures like

Hillary did in the 70s. Hillary said that she "talked to a lot of people and read the Wall Street Journal." Sounds good to me.

I can't help but think that the Clinton charitable foundation, which received over $145 million dollars from donors, didn't at least come up in dinner conversation when Hillary was Secretary of State and signing off on the Uranium One deal.

Uranium is the key element in atomic bombs. I'm probably just being overly skeptical and paranoid.

It is too bad we could not have gotten a Trump/Gingrich ticket. Instead of talking about Uranium One, the nation could focus on, and revisit, the interesting Gingrich plan to replace unionized janitors with poor children.

It is not hard to understand how our unjust system has grown so large and complicated. Just reflect on the last several United States Attorney Generals: Eric Holder, Loretta Lynch, and now Jeff Sessions. The controversies surrounding Eric Holder and Loretta Lynch are well-documented. US Attorney Sessions seems to have recused himself out of a job.

Believe it or not, I'm not trying to be political. As a convicted felon, I can't even vote. I can't, however, overlook Supreme Court Justice Ruth-Bader Ginsberg's prejudicial comments towards now President Trump during the campaign. Having some free time on my hands at Pensacola, I found that 28 USC section 455, states that any judge or magistrate judge of the United States shall disqualify herself in any proceeding in which her impartiality might reasonably be questioned. A judge is also expected to disqualify herself if she has a personal bias or prejudice concerning a party. It sounds like it's time for the other Supreme Court Justices to stage a little family intervention. Hello…. Term limits… 75 or 80 years old and OUT. She would probably have to recuse herself from First and Second Amendment arguments. I'm sure her left turn signal has been on since she left home this morning, so it should be easy to find her car in the parking lot.

How much worse can it get? Apparently, pretty bad when you look at what's happening with John Conyers, Ray Moore, Al Franken,

Bill O'Riley, Roger Ailes, Charlie Rose, and Harvey Weinstein. It's not a swamp. It's a sewer. How about our tax dollars paying for secret political sexual harassment settlements reported at more than $17 million dollars? Pretty sad.

Nearly everyone thinks that the American criminal justice system is broken and needs to be fixed. Our prisons are overflowing with men and women convicted of crimes existing only in the imagination of legislators who write the laws, and prosecutors who put as many people in prison as they can to pad their resumes. Prosecutors are not judged on how well they serve justice. They are judged by how many people they incarcerate, and how much forfeiture they generate.

If we do not strive for a legal system that addresses the whole community, we will continue to incarcerate the youth of today, and subject them to a violent and isolating environment.

According to the Justice Policy Institute, federal regulations generally limit court ordered punishments for young people. Many states, however, have recently taken advantage of waivers known as Valid Court Orders to circumvent regulations on youth incarceration. As of 2011, in more than half of the states, kids have been incarcerated for violations such as cutting class, writing graffiti on a wall, or "acting out." This incarceration pushes children into the so-called "school- to- prison" pipeline. It allows states to remove children from their communities and place them in punitive institutions.

While wealthy kids might get grounded for a week, poor kids who run away from home or defend themselves from bullies might end up jailed for the rest of their teens. Youth incarceration is linked to higher recidivism. The longer they are separated from schools and communities, the more alienated children become.

Being cut off from school could foreclose the possibility of earning a high school degree, dimming the chances of escaping the poverty that often lies at the root of the problems. The system is intrinsically cruel.

Even in sheer financial terms, imprisoning young people is unaffordable. A single young prisoner costs the state approximately $150,000 annually, according to the Justice Policy Institute.

States and cities should reinvest that money in community-based interventions providing schools with a stronger teacher workforce, hiring guidance counselors, or replacing metal detectors with midnight basketball. Early intervention could be woven throughout the social service infrastructure to keep children from slipping into destructive behavior cycles before more punitive interventions are triggered. When kids don't see a positive future path forward in life, the criminal legal system simply teaches them to be precisely what society doesn't want them to be, while denying them the right to live and learn as the children they are. Young people should be held responsible for their behavior only in a system that fulfills its own responsibility to their communities. (Portions of this section originally appeared in "In These Times".)

I never had children, but I am thankful that our church focuses on the youth.

Our pastor often says, "The future is now." Our church has made a substantial financial commitment to build an auditorium for teens to provide and build a positive atmosphere for their future growth. Hopefully, principles can be instilled that will change our community, Southwest Florida, and ultimately the world in which we live.

CHAPTER 47

———

A FRIEND ASKED ME, "HOW DOES YOUR STORY end?" The story never ends, does it? All that we have experienced continues to stream right along with no regard for beginnings or endings.

The BOP experience may be behind us, but the civil litigation continues. A couple of weeks ago, Lorie had to sit for a deposition. A date will soon be set for my deposition. The court ordered an IT technician to download all the files from my computer that has been held in court for the past two years. Most recently the plaintiffs' attorneys filed a 78-page motion for summary judgment against Lorie. I guess they now want to come and take her clothes as well. We have both had some unexpected health issues that we have had to deal with.

On August 24, 2017 we lost our little dog. He would have been 13 on September 2. He had to have his gallbladder and spleen removed, and he never fully recovered. Even with all that we've been through, this was one of the worst days ever. The heart misses most what it loved best. Sometimes I come home and find my wife crying, holding the cremated ashes of our little dog. With the ex parte order still in effect, she worries that the plaintiff's lawyers will use the order to continue their harassment by breaking into our home and taking that which we hold most dear. They had no problem taking our little dog's food during their execution of the last break order. They will have no problem taking the ashes from us at the next one.

Most recently, we were back in court requesting that the Magistrate's order denying the return of the items identified in my personal property exemption request be overturned. I had requested only a few hundred dollars of personal items that had no value to anyone else. Our request was denied. The Judge upheld the Magistrate's decision. Everyone else in the State of Florida is able to claim a personal property exemption. Apparently, I am not.

Decisions like this reaffirm what I already knew. Once you plead guilty to a felony, even after you serve your sentence, you are never allowed to fully recover. You will carry the label of "Felon" for the rest of your life. You become another valueless life in the eyes of the system. Everything stops at that point.

While our story and journey continue, I think now is as good a time as any to stop writing. I am frequently reminded of a quote from D H Lawrence, an English novelist, poet, playwright and essayist. While he died in 1930, his collected works represent, among other things, an extended reflection upon the dehumanizing effects of modernity and industrialization.

I end with one of his famous quotes. It gained some notoriety in the film "G I Jane." It is entitled "Self-Pity."

> *"I never saw a wild thing sorry for itself. A small bird will drop frozen dead from a bough without ever having felt sorry for itself."*

ACKNOWLEDGMENTS

———

I WOULD LIKE TO THANK MY FEW DEAR FRIENDS (you know who you are) who took their time to help with the editing process and keep me from running too far astray.

I would mention their names, but it is probably in their best interest that I do not.

Also, throughout my journey of incarceration, I met some really good and honorable people that became my friends. My friendships with these men are more important in my life than friends that were in my life for over 40 plus years that chose to walk away during my struggles of life. I learned a lot about people while being in "Time Out" as my mother (R.I.P) would say instead of me being in prison. Without exception I learned a lot about myself, gratitude for kindness, giving a helping hand, good belly laughs and sometimes just listening to my new friends. Some friends I met are still behind the wall and I think of them often.

Thank you, John, Jay, Roy, Ari, Steve, Chris, Captain Ron and Nick. You men were and are my wingman! God Bless you all. Everyone deserves a second chance of life!

Barb and Don, you became family in "two days!" God Bless You...we love you!

Thank you, Davide Micaro ~aka~Davide MikArt, a 29-year-old Italian boy living in Milan, Italy. He is a self-taught artist and tattoo artist with a passion for art born five years ago. He uses rich symbolism to protest society's injustice.

We are delighted to have his "Death of Freedom" art work for my book cover.

I can be contacted at sjackwilliams@gmail.com, if you would like to share your comments or relate your personal legal experiences.